YOU
ARE A GREAT &
POWERFUL
WIZARD

Self—Care Magic
for Modern Mortals

SAGE LISKEY

illustrated by Barbara Counsil

MICROCOSM PUBLISHING
Portland, Ore

YOU ARE A GREAT AND POWERFUL WIZARD

Self-Care Magic for Modern Mortals

Text © Sage Liskey, 2020
Illustrations © Barbara Counsil, 2020
This edition © Microcosm Publishing, 2020

Second edition - 3,000 copies - 7/14/2020
ISBN 978-1-62106-483-1
This is Microcosm #276

To join the ranks of high-class stores that feature Microcosm titles, talk to your local rep: In the U.S. **Como** (Atlantic), **Fujii** (Midwest), **Book Travelers West** (Pacific), **Turnaround** in Europe, **UTP/Manda** in Canada, **New South** in Australia, and **GPS** in Asia, Africa, India, South America, and other countries.

For a catalog, write or visit:
Microcosm Publishing
2752 N Williams Ave.
Portland, OR 97227
www.Microcosm.Pub

If you bought this on Amazon, I'm so sorry because you could have gotten it cheaper and supported a small, independent publisher at www.Microcosm.Pub

Library of Congress Cataloging-in-Publication Data

Names: Liskey, Sage, author. | Counsil, Barbara, illustrator.
Title: You are a great and powerful wizard : self-care magic for modern
    mortals / written by Sage Liskey ; illustrated by Barbara Counsil.
Description: Portland, Oregon : Microcosm Publishing, 2020. | Includes
    bibliographical references. | Summary: "Your words and actions have
    tremendous power. Learn how to harness that power to change your life
    and make the world a better place with this modern spell book-regardless
    of your religion or spiritual leanings. Contemporary life is confusing
    and it's easy to feel out of control. In this smart, secular witchcraft
    manual, Sage Liskey shows you how to get in touch with the mental,
    emotional, and physical aspects needed for spell casting. Chapters
    include guidance on finding your highest form, understanding your
    wizarding type, controlling your magic, overcoming roadblocks to your
    power such as depression and trauma, finding love or your ideal career,
    working with magical objects, facing a crisis, and community spell work.
    Once you've fully tapped into your magical powers, you can use them to
    effect positive change in yourself and those around you"-- Provided by
    publisher.
Identifiers: LCCN 2019051451 | ISBN 9781621064831 (paperback)
Subjects: LCSH: Witchcraft. | Magic.
Classification: LCC BF1566 .L57 2020 | DDC 133.4/3--dc23
LC record available at https://lccn.loc.gov/2019051451

MICROCOSM · PUBLISHING

Global labor conditions are bad, and our roots in industrial Cleveland in the 70s and 80s made us appreciate the need to treat workers right. Therefore, our books are MADE IN THE USA.

Microcosm Publishing is Portland's most diversified publishing house and distributor with a focus on the colorful, authentic, and empowering. Our books and zines have put your power in your hands since 1996, equipping readers to make positive changes in their lives and in the world around them. Microcosm emphasizes skill-building, showing hidden histories, and fostering creativity through challenging conventional publishing wisdom with books and bookettes about DIY skills, food, bicycling, gender, self-care, and social justice. What was once a distro and record label was started by Joe Biel in his bedroom and has become among the oldest independent publishing houses in Portland, OR. We are a politically moderate, centrist publisher in a world that has inched to the right for the past 80 years.

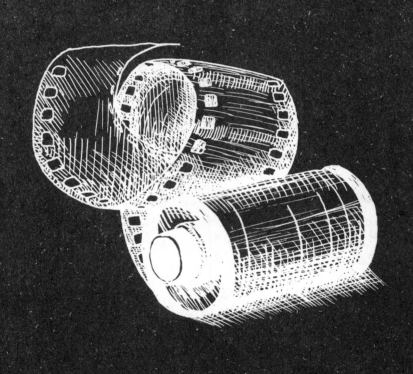

Wizard.

n; a person who changes reality.

TABLE OF CONTENTS

INTRODUCTION

hat if I told you that you are a great and powerful wizard? That magic is real? That you can love and be loved, feel fulfilled and happy, and change the world? Would you believe me?

My understanding of humanity's immense power to transform suffering, politics, culture, and reality itself began when I was young. Bullies, my father's alcoholism, my mother's depression, poverty, acne, loneliness, food sensitivities, and much more led to a deep desire for change within myself and those around me. This journey would eventually help me discover the secrets of healing my mind, body, spirit, and culture.

An especially important part of this journey was coming to realize how much of an impact a single decision can have. In 2014 I read Marshall Rosenberg's *Nonviolent Communication*. Rosenberg shares a specific method of speaking using compassion, empathy, emotion, and personal needs. Having grown up surrounded by unhealthy communication patterns, I was enthralled by the idea that such a technique existed. Around the same time I also started reading Ursula K. Le Guin's *A Wizard of Earthsea*, in which magic is cast using the "true name" of an object or person. The casting of this magic requires great study and skill, and changes depending on the region the magic is used in.

Together, these books taught me about the power of language and the cultural nuances we deal with every day to determine what we have and what we do not. Much like the wizards of Earthsea, we use these facets of language as magic spells to control our lives. Every word spoken, thought made, motion moved, and energy exchanged influences our mental state, how people perceive us, and our ability to succeed at our goals. This is magic used to make friends, fall in love, advance technologies, earn money, create art, transform habits, find happiness, influence politics, and so much more. It is the power to transform your reality and the reality of those around you.

However difficult at times, this magic is not something limited to a select few born of a special heritage. We are all great and powerful wizards capable of growth, success, overcoming suffering, and living fulfilling lives. It is intrinsic to being human that your every action is magical, each and every thing that you do or do not do creates change. Unfortunately, these abilities are rarely taught by parents or schools, and more often are seen as unimportant or are intentionally withheld to maintain power by the wizards in control. After all, a distracted, unhappy, and divided populace is easier to manipulate and exploit.

Learning to control your magic is therefore a revolutionary act, allowing you greater freedom to choose a pathway that serves you and your community best. Mastering this power is complicated. There are billions of spells being cast each moment, some reinforcing the status-quo, some preventing the success of your spells, and some weaving you a special fate far into the future. You are already under the influence of many spells, some of which serve you and others which do not. Fortunately, you have the ability to transform yourself and remove obstacles which block your way. This process will require a willingness to try, to be vulnerable, and to fail. It is all a part of understanding the essence of magic and humanity's extraordinary potential.

Suffering, while an essential part of the human experience, is felt far more frequently because of toxic beliefs and the wizards in control. You were not meant to sit in a building all day, doing work you feel distant from, with people you do not connect with, just to go home tired and questioning your existence. There is so much more beauty in this world than that.

While I still have much to learn myself, I share these spells after years of research and experiences. With this knowledge of magic I've been able to overcome obstacles, heal toxic behaviors, support loved ones, and succeed at my goals. Herein you will find spells to empower yourself, uplift your community, and transform unhealthy and destructive cultures. I hope it serves you well.

As you learn more about the wizard you are now and the wizard you would like to be in the future, you can start filling out a life map. This personal reference guide will allow you to increase your self-awareness and better understand how to obtain what you want. Each chapter ends with a series of questions to help you inquire more deeply into your highest form of being. To get the most out of your reading, it is suggested that you answer these questions in a journal. You can then further reflect on your discoveries in LIFE MAPPING, the book's final chapter.

While I have done my best to define words that are likely unfamiliar with wizards just waking up to their extensive magical powers, please see the glossary of terms at the end of this book if you need. The information contained herein has been rigorously researched in magical tomes and has worked for me, but new discoveries and insights are being made all the time. As such I do not guarantee the information's accuracy and disclaim liability for errors, omissions, and magical misfires. Furthermore, none of this is meant to be medical or legal advice.

There is much to learn. Let us begin your lessons.

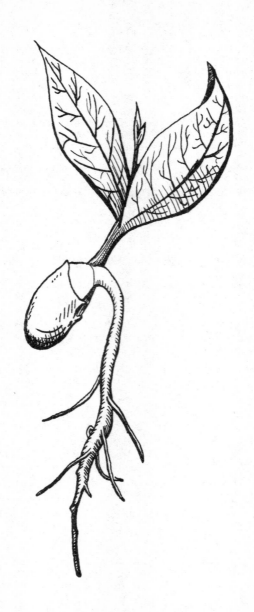

THE BASICS OF MAGIC

Magic is anything which shapes reality. This includes all physical objects, people, animals, ideas, actions, and undefined spaces which lack contents inside and outside of the universe. The *lack* of something is still influencing reality, just imagine if all space was filled! You wouldn't even be able to move. The same can be said for when we leave out certain words, keep silent, are emotionally distant, choose not to go to an event, or quiet our thoughts—that nothingness is something and has influence. That is to say, you are still using magic and changing reality, even if you are seemingly doing nothing.

In this book of spells we are concerned with understanding and controlling magic to create a desirable outcome. A wizard is a person who uses magic to intentionally transform reality. While all life and non-life is magical, humans are unique from other Earth-based lifeforms in that we individually have the greatest potential to transform reality moment to moment—it is only humans who are capable of swiftly and completely nurturing or destroying all life.

There is no good or bad magic. These concepts are constructed through the societal constructs of wizards. There is however, magic that feels better and nourishes more people. Destructive magic is relatively easy to use and can be beneficial, but each use also damages a part of yourself—anger, revenge, negative thinking, and violence will always hurt the spell caster, so you have to be careful. That is why this book primarily covers magic that heals, empowers, and transforms.

Your body, mind, soul, garments, habits, and beliefs are magic, and they can all be altered through the process of alchemy. Alchemy uses magic to transform emotions and beliefs on an individual or cultural level. It is what institutions and wizards of authority use everyday to educate or manipulate, but you can also use alchemy for yourself.

The process and actions (or lack thereof) to use magic form a magic spell. Many books of magic spells exist, also known as grimoires. These books often use descriptors such as psychology, self-help, metaphysics, communication, diet, business, spirituality, and so on to describe their magical contents. Successfully casting one of these magic spells depends on innumerable factors including: culture, language, dress, education, time of day and year, weather, and every other spell previously cast.

Some common spells people use everyday are:

- Word spells: I love you, I hate you, you're amazing, you're awful, I believe in you, you're wrong, may you have a wonderful day

- Thought spells: I'm afraid, there's no point in trying, today is a brand new day with great potential, I'm not good enough, I'm beautiful

- Movement spells: a smile, a hug, a kiss, an excited jump, a frown, a snicker, a glare, laughter

- Energy spells: clearing your mind of all thoughts or judgment, praying for someone, asking for forgiveness, embodying a sense of revenge and hatred, embracing joy and love, naming an object, cleaning up your room

These can be further broken down into spells you consciously cast and spells you subconsciously cast (see THE SUBCONSCIOUS). Subconscious spells are cast automatically and without your awareness. They are heavily influenced by what has filled your subconscious landscape throughout your life such as the communication style your parents used, the media you consume, and your friends. Conscious spells are the ones you deliberately cast.

Beyond the spells inherent to an individual, there are also magic potions and objects. Magic potions like food, water, medicine, air, and other consumables alter the mind and body's chemical composition. Magical objects include garments, tools, antiques, and other material items which alter a person or group's magic potential.

Each person holds the potential to use magic and transform reality. A wizard's basic magic potential is determined by their ability to use words, thoughts, movements, and energy within a given environment. Equipping yourself with various wizardly possessions (MAGICAL

OBJECTS), befriending magical allies (GROUP SPELLS AND MAGICAL ALLIES), consuming particular substances (MAGIC POTIONS), and having new experiences (QUESTS) may then be used to further increase this potential.

Wizards have a dynamic magic potential—it can quickly grow or shrink depending on a variety of influences. Growing your potential increases your ability to successfully cast simple and complicated magic spells. Even wizards with a seemingly infinite potential are still bound by the spells of other wizards and their physical limitations.

Once you believe you have enough magic potential to cast a particular spell, you can go through the casting process. Many aspects of reality cannot be controlled by a single word or motion. Most magical effects may only be obtained by weaving together different types of spells and wizards. Spells usually increase in complexity and difficulty as the desired effects seek to influence more of a target's time and energy. For instance, making wizards smile is relatively simple, whereas convincing one to fall in love with you takes careful weaving of words, movements, thoughts, and feelings together. When you know you do not have the ability or desire to cast a spell, you can seek help from magical allies (see GROUP SPELLS AND MAGICAL ALLIES). The success of your spells are also dependent upon learning to control your magic and your personal wizard type.

Your wizard type includes your personality, cultural viewpoint, and general brain chemistry. Wizards across the world are immensely diverse, but also share basic needs including: sustenance, safety, love, empathy, rest, community, creativity, freedom, and purpose. These aspects of ourselves are natural and intrinsic to being human. On the other hand, there is a myriad of personality traits and desires which are nurtured into us through our culture, or wizarding clan. A wizard clan is a group of people tied together through shared beliefs, nationality, race, language, dress, and so on.

Each clan uses a unique set of magic spells and passes that onto their youth through parenting, schooling, and societal pressure. This cultural identity forms close bonds between the people belonging to clans. These spells are however, not static—especially now with so many wizard clans interacting. It is also possible to create entirely new clans, but getting the culture to spread widely can be difficult with how ideologically saturated the world is. Note that achieving the same spell effects on individuals belonging to two different clans may require using entirely different spells for each. It is therefore essential you have an understanding of various types of wizards and clans.

. . .

Life Mapping

What types of magic are you skilled with and which do you feel some difficulty around? What are some big spells you have had success at casting? What spells have you failed to cast? What type of magic would you like to become more skilled with?

CONTROLLING YOUR MAGIC

Many wizard clans do not teach their children the specifics of using magic to cast spells, instead assuming that they will figure it out on their own or are too young to understand. This is incredibly dangerous, because as these young wizards mature into adults, they have little control over of the spells they are casting. Each of your words, thoughts, movements, and energies are transforming you and the surrounding world, but is that magic intentionally beneficial or accidentally hurtful?

An important step in mastering magic is becoming aware of the impact your spells create. Awareness requires knowledge and knowledge requires study. This knowledge is best obtained through hands-on experience and research, but hearing the personal accounts of old and deceased wizards may also work. When you practice magic, there will be times that you fail, but one of the greatest teachers is failure, so be vulnerable—there will usually be more opportunities to try again. Consider when practicing magic:

- There are many ways to create the same spell effects.

- Some magic will only work in the right time and place.

- Your spell effects are especially influenced by the greater pool of magic being cast by other wizards.

- Magic that is negative or destructive to the user often casts without your awareness. Be careful.

- A spell need not make any logical sense as it may tap into the emotional, subconscious, and spiritual mind. So long as it works, that is enough.

- Some spells are harder to control than others. These spells require a lot of training to cast properly and may need to be periodically recast to work effectively.

- Many spell effects are contagious—despair will cause others to feel despair, while embodying love will make others feel love.

- The world is complex and takes time to understand. The most successful wizards not only try multiple times, they also try using different strategies until one works.

Growing Your Magic Potential

As previously mentioned, magic potential determines your capacity to cast spells, especially ones of great power and reach. The potential to successfully cast a spell is influenced by a huge number of factors and can quickly fluctuate depending on the spells cast by other wizards. Inherently, as a human you are capable of incredibly powerful magic, however a handful of factors can exponentially influence your potential at a local, regional, national, or world-wide level. These include:

- Being part of a particular wizard clan.

- Your level of self-confidence.

- Gaining status among a group of people, such as with a political position, doing well at a job, or destroying or creating something that people appreciate.

- How attractive your appearance is to a person.

- Working jobs or having certain skills that are respected in a wizard clan.

- Having a small or large amount of money.

- Having possession of certain wizarding equipment.

- Volunteering or making donations to causes.

- Being well-liked or being despised.

- Knowing how a particular wizard clan wants to be communicated with.

- Having a mental or physical ailment.

- Having certain freedoms revoked.

By considering your current situation in life, you can begin to determine what aspects grow and what aspects drain your magic potential. Losing a source of potential can be difficult, but may actually help you find new or different sources of it in the future. For instance, ending a relationship or quitting a job may temporarily decrease your magic potential, but opens you up to finding stronger and healthier sources of it as well.

Also, performing actions a group of people dislike may increase your potential in certain ways, but it will also decrease it in others. For instance, being a bully will give you power and notoriety, but will also make people less willing to be your friend or support you when in need. Generally, it's better to try to get along with people rather than being divisive. Of course, how much an action is appreciated changes significantly between different wizard clans and individuals, so you need to know how aspects of your personality resonate with different people. If you are having trouble growing your magic potential, you may need to relearn the basics of magic by changing your wizard type or working on your mental health.

Study

In order to boost your magical awareness, study a wide variety of humanistic subjects like psychology, communication, and art. Put yourself among many unique types of wizards from all over the world, as each wizard is a guru that you have something to learn from. Apply to jobs, seek out new relationships, defeat old habits, or go to a country with an unfamiliar language. These experiences will help you understand the many types of spells that exist in the world and how to cast them. More than anything, a wizard needs practice and experience.

Open Your Mind

Your studies require an open mind. A great wizard is adept in believing the truths of each wizard clan, seeing their ideologies as equal. Initially it is not your place to negate what others believe. Instead practice being each of these unique personalities. Walk in their shoes and be able to hold two or more contradicting viewpoints in your mind at once. This will assist you in understanding the myriad of realities that wizards exist within, each valid to its own clan. Learning the nuances of a clan's culture will also help you start to see when a reality is unlikely to be true due to hypocrisy. Together, studying and opening your mind will give you the ability to transform your habits and decide which spells you want to be using.

Habits and Autocasting Magic Spells

Habits are repetitive and sometimes subconsciously cast magic spells (see THE SUBCONSCIOUS). Extended periods of a mental state such as being sad, anxious, or depressed may even cause the state to become habitual and more easily appear in the future.

According to wizard Charles Duhigg, a habit has three parts to it: the "habit cues," the habit itself, and the reward for performing the habit (*Gross 2012*). An example would be the smell of cookies (the habit cue), leading you to purchase and eat a cookie (the habit), which in turn temporarily boosts your dopamine and satisfies your sweet tooth (the reward). Habit cues may include sights, sounds, smells, feelings, or memories of these things. Once the habit has initiated, the brain actually automates the magic spell and is free to think about other thoughts and actions.

Everyone forms habits at different rates, though three weeks has become a popularized average time frame (*Layton*). If you are performing a spell regularly enough, it should stay permanently wired within your neural makeup after this amount of time (*Delude 2005*). This is great for healthy habits, but also makes breaking an unhealthy habit exceptionally difficult. Even if you do break a habit, being around old habit cues can quickly make the habit reform and old spells start firing unconsciously again (*Gross 2012*). This is especially challenging as the rewards for an unhealthy behavior are often more immediate than the rewards for healthy behaviors. So how can you transform these types of spells into new habits?

Tips for Forming Habits:

- Repeat the behavior often and at regular intervals.

- Start small. Form one habit at a time, and perform that habit a few times a week rather than every day.

- Schedule the habit, with specifics of when and for how long. For instance, for 30 minutes on Mondays, Wednesdays, and Fridays at 9:00AM I will _____ . work or life schedule shifts around, make a time reference to accommodate it, such as "when I get off work" or "after I eat dinner."

- Make the reward for the habit visible. Keep a daily log of how you feel from performing the habit, or treat yourself to something nice (but healthy!) for accomplishing the behavior.

- Make a game out of the activity, either competing against yourself or other people. Games greatly increase motivation.

- Work on forming the habit with someone else, such as an exercise buddy. This way you will both feel obligated to not skip your exercise schedule. You can also seek help through counselors, therapists, and support groups.

- Use any number of smartphone apps for forming habits with.

- If you are not motivated to do a healthy activity, try thinking of why you're doing it in a more involved way. For instance, "to love my whole body," "to document magic," "to get away from those silly humans," "to get artistic inspiration," or "to see my tree friends."

- Make good habits more visible. For instance, put supplements next to your bed, healthy foods on the kitchen counter, or a book you should read in your bag.

- Force yourself to do it. It may be uncomfortable, but really, you're never going to want to do something you don't feel motivated to do, or have yet to create a habit for. As wizard Amy Cuddy says, "fake it till you make it."

Tips for Deforming Habits:

- Food, drugs, alcohol, and other addictions are often the result of stress, so in order to deform these types of habits, you may have to first create a more stable and calm life for yourself (*Sinha 2013*).

- Recognize the "habit cues" and rewards for a given habit. This will give you some power over the habit, understanding how it is initiated and where it is coming from.

- If a "habit cue" such as stress or seeing junk food causes you to perform an unhealthy habit, train yourself to perform a healthy habit when you receive those habit cues instead. For instance, if you smell cookies, instead of going to eat the cookies, do push-ups, or breathe deeply. People also will wear a rubber band on their wrist and snap it any time a habit cue arises, thus providing a distraction and bringing you back into the present moment.

- Remove unhealthy "habit cues" from your life if possible, even if it means ending a friendship or changing your living space.

- Change your environment. The easiest way to alter a habit is by doing so on vacation or moving to a new place, because you are removed from the "habit cues" of your normal environment. *(Gross 2012)*.

- Put the habit just a little further out of reach so you think twice before initiating it. For instance, temporarily block websites with a blocking program, place an addicting food out of sight, or use a time lock safe to secure a device from yourself for a set period of time.

- In order to prevent businesses from making you eat unhealthy food or compulsively buying their goods, understand how colors, smells, language, and advertisements are used to manipulate your purchasing decisions. Also learning about nutrition, malnourishment, and preventable diseases will give you further reason to make healthier eating choices. This education can be especially influential in children and teenagers.

- Write brief statements over and over about your rationale for ending a habit and how that habit negatively impacts you.

- Read this list periodically or whenever you fall back into an unhealthy habit.

Successful Magic

The success of a magic spell is determined by the intentions of the caster or wizard clan. A successful magic spell will meet certain criteria of your original desires—but often to complete a spell's influence, several more spells will have to be woven together to stabilize the effects sought out. A spell will only be successful in ideal conditions, such as with the time of day, surrounding culture, magical objects used, potions consumed, environment, time of year, spells other wizards have been casting, type of wizard you are dealing with, and so on. An unsuccessful spell is a great learning opportunity; perhaps it tells you more about the type of wizard the other person is, perhaps it tells you about where your spells could use improvement, or perhaps it teaches you something in general about life. Failure is the greatest guru.

Some wizards would argue that success and failure do not exist, for this duality is merely of human invention, outside the realms of nature. Don't get too upset if you are unsuccessful in casting a spell. The past and future matter, but most important is this moment. What if casting an unsuccessful magic spell is part of weaving a much greater spell that positively transforms your life? What if your success in casting a spell ultimately leads to your demise? There is no way of knowing, so all you can do is keep learning.

Typically spells will have a much greater chance of success when utilizing a wizard's basic biology and needs. There are certain senses that all wizards desire. For instance, it is more likely that a person will enjoy your cooking if the food is salty, fatty, or sweet. There are also the needs a person has for things like freedom, safety, friendship, love, and entertainment, that if incorporated into your spells, will greatly help your success.

Keep in mind that all creation leads to destruction and all destruction leads to creation. Furthermore, there is no definitive "good" or "bad" magic, only the will of the wizard or clan casting a spell. A powerful wizard knows how to use magic in order to achieve destruction or creation that is beneficial to their personal wizardly ambitions.

• • •

Life Mapping

How much control do you have over your magic? What actions can you take to gain better control over it? What habits do you currently live with? What habits do you want to form and how are you going to go about changing unwanted habits? What are your primary sources of magic potential? How could you gain more magic potential?

TYPES OF MAGIC

Knowing the type of wizard that you are and what sort of wizard you are attempting to cast magic on will greatly assist you in choosing the proper spell to use. Wizards may be categorized in many ways, each with useful snippets of information. Your wizard type may change considerably depending on if you look at your internal or external self, as well as what wizard clan you interact with. For instance a wizard might be internally anxious but outwardly aggressive, or joyful with friends but quiet around strangers. Wizards may also knowingly or unknowingly wear personality masks, which convey them as being one wizardly type when in fact they are another. These masks are often worn out of self-protection and may prevent you from being the person you really want to be.

The types of wizard you identify as are flexible. If one wizarding type is not serving you any longer, you can revoke old patterns and learn new ones. This is harder with behaviors inherited from growing up in a particular wizard clan, but still possible. The only thing in the way is your personal attachment to who you identify as. You may also receive backlash for becoming a wizard type that goes against the culture of a dominant wizard clan. Changing your wizard type is a good idea when, for instance, you seemingly cannot make friends, get a job, find happiness, or become romantically engaged with a person.

Some people experience confusion and suffering surrounding a loss of their wizarding type. Identity crises may result from a myriad of changes you or others undergo. The loss of an identity can be thought of as an exciting opportunity to create an even better, stronger, and truer you, or simply to try out a different way of life.

Time is an important component of finding a new identity or re-finding an identity. It usually will not happen overnight, especially when friends and family try to reinforce your old patterns. It is therefore important to inform family and old friends of your changes, as well as to find new friends, community, and activities to engage in for support developing your new identity (see FORMING MAGICAL ALLIES under GROUP SPELLS AND MAGICAL ALLIES).

It will also be helpful to explore yourself through writing, and create a plan of what your new identity looks like. To move forward you might also need to release everything from the past and live wholly in the present moment, move locations, or hold a ritual or ceremony for your change (see MAGICAL ACTIVITIES).

Your Wizardly Personality

One great way to begin exploring your wizard types is by taking various personality tests. Humans have difficulty seeing their own personality, and so finding ways to reflect your inward and outward traits is important. No personality test will expose the full spectrum of who you are or be 100% accurate, but the results will give you ideas you can take from. There are many different personality tests and below are some of the most popular which can be taken online.

Big Five

The Big Five is generally seen as one of the most scientifically accurate of personality tests. It gauges a person's openness to experience, conscientiousness, extraversion, agreeableness, and neuroticism.

Myers-Briggs Type Indicator (MBTI)

The Myers-Briggs Type Indicator was developed by wizards Katharine Cook Briggs and Isabel Briggs Myers and is based on Carl Jung's wizarding research and theories. The personality types are broken down into four categories with two types each—extroverted or introverted, sensing or intuitive, thinking or feeling, and judging or perceiving. The MBTI is often criticized as unscientific, but the results often resonate with people and are much easier to casually talk about with friends than the Big Five.

Astrology

There are many types of astrology around the world. Western Astrology uses a person's date of birth, where they were born, and celestial alignment to assign one of twelve primary zodiac signs and a myriad of secondary ones to create an extensive personality chart. Different astrologers then write daily, weekly, monthly, or yearly horoscopes which correspond to a person's zodiac signs. These horoscopes give advice or foretell events to come. Even if you don't believe in astrology, they can still be a useful way for seeking out unique wisdom and new ways of looking at your life.

Others

There are many more personality tests. The enneagram, Jungian Archetypes, numerology, media quizzes like the Harry Potter Sorting Hat, and so on, all help illuminate hidden aspects of yourself. Seek them out to unravel the mystery of who you are.

Introverts and Extroverts

There are distinctive social differences between introverts, extroverts, and shy people, and it is worth exploring which trait(s) you tend toward. Wizard Susan Cain's New York Times bestseller, *Quiet*, describes these personalities quite well. Debate exists over the exact definitions of introvert and extrovert, but the basic idea is that introverts need more alone time or quieter one-on-one social interaction to recharge their energy, whereas extroverts find social life and groups energizing (*Cain 2013*).

Everyone is on a spectrum between an introvert and extrovert, with few people fully taking on all the characteristics of one category. An ambivert has some tendencies of both. The United States of America is actually dominated by extroverted thought in schools, work spaces, and culture, even though at least one third of the population consists of introverts. This means that many people are being forced into overwhelming environments which do not allow them to perform to their best ability.

If someone is introverted, it does not mean that they dislike groups or social interaction. In fact, introverts can thrive in extroverted environments, they just might periodically need alone time to energetically recharge. For an overwhelmed introvert these might include places like their room, nature, a quiet space with one other friend, or a bathroom stall. Even just putting on headphones and playing some music over the bustle of the world can help.

Both introverts and extroverts can experience shyness, a trait describing social anxiety or hesitation toward strangers, acquaintances, and even friends. Unfortunately, introverts are more likely to experience depression than extroverts due to a tendency of obsessively thinking over the same thought (*Law 2005*). Many introverts share characteristics including:

- Enjoyment of solitude or one-on-one interactions
- Dislike of small talk, risk-taking, and conflict
- Better at listening than talking

- Work best alone and without interruption
- Socially quieter than extroverts
- Highly creative, intelligent, and thoughtful
- Expresses oneself best through mediums such as writing or art instead of public speaking or group activities
- Prefers friendly people over argumentative or conflict-oriented people
- Easily feels guilty
- Has trouble multitasking
- Has trouble accurately reading emotions and social cues during interactions with others

Extroverts on the other hand often:
- Enjoy talking and being the center of attention
- Get energized from one-on-one or group interactions
- Act first and think later
- Have many friends
- Are happier than introverts
- Dislike too much alone time
- Seek out ideas and solutions from others
- Are energetic and feel comfortable being loud
- Make lots of body motions and sounds
- Are the first to speak up

Introverts also tend to fit the category of "highly sensitive." Highly sensitive wizards have to be careful about trying to protect themselves too much from the world or slightly uncomfortable things, because doing so may prevent their ability to have any new experiences. According to Wizard Elaine Aron, people with high sensitivities often:

- Have strong observational skills

- Avoid surprises

- Experience exterior stimuli powerfully

- Become anxious or underperform when others watch or judge them

- Notice emotional changes in others

- Have strong empathetic feelings

- Avoid unempathetic situations such as violent media

Learning Styles

There are several methods of receiving information, with some wizards learning best with one method over another. You'll have to experiment to see which you prefer and which keeps your attention, but learning styles can be broken down into three types:

- Kinesthetic: Absorbs information with hands-on experiences likes games, hikes, and step-by-step tutorials.

- Auditory: Great at listening to information like lectures and podcasts.

- Visual: Best educated with visual mediums such as videos, presentation slides, infographics, and comics.

Intelligence

Intelligence is a wizard's ability to both acquire new knowledge and use existing knowledge to obtain a desirable outcome. There are different types of intelligences that makes various aspects of magic easier to understand and use. Wizard Howard Gardener includes in this list:

- Linguistic: words, speaking, writing, and memorizing
- Logical-Mathematical: problem-solving and abstract ideas
- Naturalist: botany and an enjoyment of being in nature
- Visual-Spatial: design and can see easily see patterns
- Bodily-Kinesthetic: experiential, hands-on, sports, and dance
- Musical: attune to sound, rhythm, and making music
- Interpersonal: social and engages easily with others
- Intrapersonal: emotions, self-reflection, self-aware

You can increase your intelligence in any given area through practice in a related skill, but depending on other components of your wizarding type and how that field was initially introduced to you, some intelligences will come easier than others.

Age

With some children being much more capable and wiser than older wizards, a person's abilities and intelligence can rarely be determined through how many years they have been on the planet. However, there are many biochemical changes that take place throughout life that can be important to know about.

Pre-Borns

A child's well-being begins before birth, in the womb. Parents' genes mingle together in determining many physical and mental aspects of a baby. Genes can even pass on stress and trauma experienced by the parents. However, gene expression can at least be partly dictated by upbringing, so raising children in a healthy environment can mitigate some of these factors. Even better is to take care of yourself before having a child. Beyond genes, pregnant wizards who eat a proper diet are much more likely to give birth on time and to a baby with a healthy weight, two factors linked to youth happiness and better cognitive ability later in life.

Infants

Babies raised on breast milk receive an important balance of essential fatty acids linked to proper brain development. Keep in mind that anything consumed, including medicines, will be present in breast milk, and some of these things are not healthy for young ones. Children and pregnant people do have different nutritional requirements than others, so if possible, you should do your research before caring for a child or becoming pregnant.

Wizards may be greatly influenced by the time of year they were born. In one study, summer children were found to have greater mood swings, but along with spring children, were happier (*European College of Neuropsychopharmacology 2014*). People born in the winter were less irritable, but more depressed. Fall children experienced less depression than those born in the winter. This is likely due to fluctuations in a mother's hormones and stress levels through the year being passed onto a child.

More directly, anything that happens around a baby or child will greatly influence their behaviors and personality later. Young ones benefit from being raised with lots of positive touch, colorful and artistic environments with many items to play with, and parents who are in control of their own emotional well-being so as to use love and patience rather than anger and abuse.

Children

Children are extremely creative and smart, but do not have much concept of right and wrong due to being driven primarily by emotional urges rather than rational thought. Children take after their surroundings, which largely falls upon the actions of their parents.

In part due to their emotional nature, children can begin forming addictions to things they really like and usually do not have the foresight that it might be harmful. While children need a good amount of freedom to discover and learn about the world on their own, some healthy guidance is essential as well.

Teens

Puberty starts as a teenager, throwing the mind into a wild cycle of hormonal shifts and (often repressed) sexual interests. Unfortunately this transition is made especially difficult by the lack of education given by parents and society to help teens to cope properly. This is further exacerbated by teenagers being granted little power to determine their own pathway as they face oppression from their family, age, schooling expectations, and location, potentially resulting in emotionally troubled times. Wizards of this age often feel stifled by these factors, but will flourish when treated with respect and given some authority over their life. You can read more about raising kids in FAMILY under GROUP SPELLS AND MAGICAL ALLIES.

Adults

The brain doesn't fully develop until at least the age of 25, with major changes in hormones and the prefrontal cortex. This region of the brain is responsible for socializing, personality, and making decisions. Wizards with developed brains are better at creating plans and are less likely to do risky things. These "grown-ups" generally need to start earning enough money to afford basic needs, entertainment, and a variety of magical objects and services to increase their well-being and spell casting power. During this search, many wizards seek out educational assistance and develop one or several passions to pursue, though not everyone is able to combine their passion with job profession. Many others forget about their passion or never get around to pursuing it in the struggle to obtain money (see DESTRUCTIVE SPELLS THAT WIZARDS ARE COMMONLY UNDER and BUSINESS under MAGIC ALCHEMY).

As adults settle into patterns, their sense of time speeds up. This is because time slows as you have more unique experiences, and speeds up as you start repeating old experiences. No matter what, time will move faster for adults than it does for children because the world is completely new to young ones whereas adults will have already mastered many of the essential aspects of survival. That said, it can be slowed, so long as adult wizards keep learning and pursuing unknown experiences, or vary their life enough to keep old experiences fresh and exciting.

Aged Wizards

Aged wizards may be free to explore and celebrate life at their leisure. There are places to go, stories to tell, and people to keep in touch with. That said, growing older also comes with many trials. These include hormonal changes, physical changes, weakening of the body, a greater risk of life-threatening diseases, difficulty understanding youth culture and new technologies, seeing loved ones pass away, and being confronted with death. This can create a lot of stress and loneliness, especially as the body breaks down and is unable to enjoy old habits. This phase of life is often reflected by everything a person has done over their lifespan and is generally more enjoyable when they have eaten right, exercised, and continuously learned new things.

Relationships

Single people, couples, and parents all carry different energies. Single people are often seeking personal fulfillment. Couples are steered by their relationship dynamics, whether that be codependent and closed off or open to outside touch and sharing friends and lovers. Parents often exist almost solely for their children with less time to pursue personal interests. See more in ROMANCE and FAMILY under GROUP SPELLS AND MAGICAL ALLIES.

Sexual Interests

Wizards have many types of sexual interests including different genders or sexes (heterosexual), the same gender or sex (homosexual), multiple genders or sexes (bisexual), all genders or sexes (pansexual), particular actions (kinks), or certain objects (objectophilia). A person might also not experience sexual feelings at all (asexual). These interests may change over a person's lifetime.

Relationship Dynamics

There are many forms of romantic relationships. Covered broadly, they include:

- Aromantic wizards—do not experience romantic attraction, but can still have platonic (non-sexual) love.

- Monogamous wizards—are only interested in having one sexual partner at a time, but this often includes limiting all forms of positive touch, like holding hands, to a single person.

- Polyamorous wizards—are open to having multiple sexual partners, or at least one sexual partner and multiple people who share positive touch with them. Polyamory often necessitates more communication and reduces the risk of codependent relationships, but can also increase jealousy and be quite complicated. It is based on the idea that no one person is capable of meeting all of your needs, including romantic ones.

- Some wizards are also only interested in uncommitted relationships and having casual sex, while others want some security in a committed agreement.

Political Orientation

Wizards often align their personality and needs with a political belief. This can range between having rule under authority versus freedom under a lack of rules, and collective work versus individual determination. Political orientation may be determined through religious affiliation, level of trust in government, economic level, priority given to the individual or common good, and many other factors.

Basis for Truth

Most wizards use science, spirituality, religion, or a combination of all three to determine what is fundamentally true. Science uses observations and experiments conducted with the five primary senses to determine truth with, and as such can be replicable worldwide by anyone with the correct tools. These truths are always open to change should new discoveries be made. Religion and spirituality rely on personal feelings, the words of leaders, the experiences of individuals, and believing in energies not immediately observable by everyone. As religion and spirituality are often founded by long-deceased individuals or groups with specific rules for proper behavior as a member, they tend not to change as much as science does. Due to this inflexibility and people continuing to have new spiritual experiences and ideas on how to be better at their religious practices, a diverse array of belief structures have risen.

Gender

Gender is defined differently between various wizard clans. Some use it to mean the same thing as a person's genitals. Others determine a wizard's gender by how that wizard outwardly displays their personality and appearance compared to other wizards of the same sex or gender within a culture. Still others believe that gender is a myriad of choices without much bearing on your appearance or personality. And then there are wizards who believe that gender creates needless divisions, is meaningless, or doesn't exist at all.

Gender identity can create many strong feelings when different wizard clans interact. In general you should be aware that throughout the world and history there are many ideas about gender and wizards may demand to have specific pronouns used such as he, she, they, zie, just a name, or a number of others regardless of what you perceive their gender to be. On the other hand, many wizards will demand to use certain pronouns for you depending on their wizard clan. Misgendering or refusing to use a wizard's pronouns is offensive and should be avoided at all costs. Wizards with genders unfamiliar to you will be much happier and friendlier if you respect them.

Brain Chemistry

Good mental health is vital to using magic effectively and is marked by having the ability to take care of your basic physical and mental needs. Everyone's brains are different and perceive reality in completely unique ways. This difference can act as a super power for some, and a great hindrance to others. How these wizards are treated and cope depends on the culture they belong to, how much control they have over their magic, and whether or not they receive support. Usually these brain chemistries can stabilize with a supportive and healthy community, but that is rarely available in many modern wizard communities.

Ask a doctor for resources that address your personal chemistry if you are having trouble adapting to certain environments or struggling with difficult emotions. Some of the most common brain chemistries that may lead to these outcomes include aspergers and autism, attention deficit/hyperactive disorder (ADHD), depression and trauma, manic depression (bipolar), schizophrenia, and Tourette's syndrome. While some people feel stigmatized by these labels, many others are able to find coping mechanisms and support for what may be making their life difficult.

Of these brain chemistries, almost all wizards will one day face depression, with the condition having many unique causes, symptoms, and solutions. It is essentially an extended period of mental suffering. There are many sub-categories of depression which can cause things like anxiety, trouble sleeping and apathy. Even then, simply saying that someone has depression is misleading, because everyone experiences it uniquely on a spectrum. Depression is one of the most common blockades to becoming a powerful wizard, so I address the topic thoroughly throughout this book. See COPING WITH THE DARKNESS for the causes of depression and methods of effectively dealing with the condition.

Cultural Identity

A wizard's clan primes them from birth to talk, act, and believe a certain way. It is useful to at least have a vague idea of what a wizard's clan instills in their members. Wizards from different cultures vary in how they interact with one another. Holidays, religious and spiritual beliefs, and trust in science also change depending on culture. Naturally, in this era of cultural diversity, you can't always know for certain how a person's culture reflects their personality, so avoid making assumptions. When unsure of your clan's or someone else's cultural traditions, ask, but also keep in mind that not everyone feels comfortable sharing this information with a stranger. There are also some wizards who belong to no clan and are open-minded or apathetic about culture and what they believe in.

In interacting with a diversity of cultures, it is good to learn about the histories and traumas of a group of wizards as it relates to your own. Perhaps your race or nation discriminated against or did terrible things to another wizarding clan and it is hard for them to accept your presence. Or, perhaps you are much loved and celebrated but there are other antagonists. Knowing ahead of time can prime you to use the right magic spells and not trigger any hard feelings.

Income Level

Different income levels can have various effects on a wizard. Growing up poor increases the potential of experiencing depression, while having a higher income is associated with greater emotional well-being (Kim 2013). Poorer wizards, however, tend to be more giving with their money. Many people lose themselves in unhappy jobs for the pursuit of higher income, but dislike the work and have no life outside of increasing earnings. Money can bring a lot of comfort to life, but so can a fulfilling job and healthy work environment.

Education Level

What sort of education a wizard receives or seeks out greatly influences the type of reasoning they use to determine their personal sense of truth. It has also traditionally correlated with their income and general well-being, but this may be changing as many wizards teach themselves through alternative means of education such as online videos, tutorials, and forums. Read more in SCHOOL under DESTRUCTIVE SPELLS THAT WIZARDS ARE COMMONLY UNDER.

Disabilities

Physical and mental disabilities force many people to go through life differently than those without them. Disabilities are not always apparent, but may result in movements, speech, reading, socializing, and general cognitive abilities becoming difficult or costly in time and energy. With proper accessibility, wizards with disabilities can still travel, learn, and socialize on their own. Unfortunately, many places do not have these options, resulting in a greater amount of isolation, worsening of conditions, or depression. Wizards with disablities may also experience discrimination in the workplace and public for being seen as different, and generally have struggles that most people are unfamiliar with.

Leaders and Followers

Some wizards prefer to lead others, either with their unique ideas or perpetuating spells cast long ago. These wizards may be addicted to money and power, or have a deep desire to create change. Other wizards prefer to follow and live their life out in systems created by others. These wizards can have much more personal time, but may find themselves easily manipulated or fall under the control of destructive spells. You can learn more about leaders and followers under THE WIZARDS IN CONTROL in DESTRUCTIVE SPELLS WIZARDS ARE COMMONLY UNDER.

•   •   •

Life Mapping

What are your wizard types? Which of these benefit you and which do not? Are there any types of wizards you aspire to become?

THE SUBCONSCIOUS

I f you want to know your wizard type and control your magic on an even deeper level, you have to learn about the subconscious. When we use magic, or magic is used on us, it targets the conscious or subconscious mind. Your conscious self includes the mindful decisions you make to speak, express yourself, and actively choose between various options. However, there is another level of self which works underneath your active awareness and impacts your life in more fundamental and intricate ways. This subconscious self is responsible for all actions, thoughts, beliefs, and emotions performed without your conscious input. This includes things like emotions, self-limiting thoughts, movements, and habits thus accounting for the majority of your spells cast throughout the day.

For many aspects of magic, there is actually little difference between the waking life, dreams, and imagination because they are all unified by your subconscious world. In other words, any of these spaces can grant you great meaning, help you learn new spells, heal emotional and spiritual wounds, and untangle yourself from the darkness. They can also cause you great suffering and diminish your magical energy if you do not gain proper control over them. For instance, yelling at someone in your imagination will cause you to feel angry and stressed out, just as if you did it in real life. If a monster attacks you in your dreams, you will wake feeling fearful of the world, and may even feel pain in your body.

That being said, the waking life, dreams, and imagination can engage different levels of the subconscious.

The Formation of Subconscious Actions

It is incredibly difficult to realize how any given spell is transforming you—the media, ads, and cultures you consume change you in small ways over time. What does witnessing violence do to you? Or listening to angry music? Or seeing the same logo everywhere? Or not being around enough nature? You don't realize the influence these things are having on you, but they are all having an accumulative impact.

Some subconscious actions are inherent to all humans, but will be expressed uniquely depending on your personal life factors. Many other subconscious actions form under specific criteria. Depending on the situation, a single significant event or a repetition of similar events may change the way your subconscious behaves in the world. For instance, being frightened by a dog as a child may make you dislike dogs as an adult. Consuming media over a period of time in which a particular body type is depicted may make you more attracted to that body type. Being raised in a household that uses cynical humor may give rise to you laughing at cynical humor. When these thoughts and feelings become reinforced enough, they can turn into deeply ingrained beliefs which dictate the shape of your reality.

Your Subconscious Behaviors

The shape of your subconscious actions can be observed through careful inquiry into your dreams, emotions, habits, fears, beliefs, desires, memories, and creative outlets. What patterns can you see in how others treat you when you act or react? Has someone ever communicated a reflection of how you come off in the world that you were unaware of? These are facets of your subconscious personality.

Anything you consciously or unconsciously sense or think of, starting in the womb, becomes permanently added to your subconscious landscape, but may also include feelings and fears inherited from your parents. Not every addition changes your behavior directly, but may overtime; so when possible, be careful with what you are putting into your brain. Unfortunately, because subconscious actions can form before your memory develops, it can be quite difficult to pinpoint why you act in certain ways. Speaking with your parents, relatives, and their friends about your family's history may help explain some of your subconscious behaviors.

Your Shadow and Light Forms

One useful way of working on your subconscious is by splitting it into shadow and light forms. Your shadow form includes the aspects of your subconscious responsible for destructive spells like your judgments, self-doubts, regrets, hypocritical actions, addictions, shortcomings, and other things that may lead to a negative mindset or consume you with darkness. Even though these may be aspects of yourself you eventually seek to work on, they are still part of your humanity and are not evil. In fact, your shadow form can be quite beneficial by allowing you to learn from your past mistakes, strive to be better, understand the darkness, keep you safe, and empathize with the shadows of others. In this way, wizards with more developed shadow forms are able to gain greater insight into the realm of magic.

On the other hand, your light form is responsible for your creative spells including things like love, laughter, a sense of friendship, caring, and joy. These subconscious reactions typically feel nourishing, but are not always healthy or expressed in a way that is beneficial to you in the long term. For instance, loving someone can be hurtful to you or the person involved, or you might laugh at a joke, but that joke might belittle someone else. Regardless, your light form is capable of filling you with happiness and fulfillment.

When people talk about altering these aspects of themselves, they use the terms "shadow work" or "light work." Both your shadow and light forms are important aspects of yourself, and need each other to form a healthy you. In analyzing your subconscious, look at the behaviors in your life which uplift and depress you. How are these beneficial, destructive, or not serving you? Are there certain behaviors belonging to your shadow or light that would be useful to change? What new aspects would you like them to take on?

Altering Subconscious Behaviors

Since subconscious behaviors are performed without your conscious input, they can be difficult to alter once formed, but you are a great and powerful wizard so the task is quite possible. This topic has already been partly covered in HABITS AND AUTOCASTING MAGIC SPELLS under CONTROLLING YOUR MAGIC, but let's take a look at how it applies specifically to the subconscious. You can also learn about rewiring the subconscious behavioral patterns of others in ACTIVISM AND ALCHEMIZING THE MAGIC OF OTHER WIZARDS under MAGIC ALCHEMY.

Your primary tool for altering subconscious behaviors will be your conscious self. With it, you can deflect spells from becoming entangled in your subconscious (see DESTRUCTIVE SPELLS THAT WIZARDS ARE COMMONLY UNDER), as well as rewiring subconscious behaviors already there. This is most easily done through repetition, which responds well to either punishment for unwanted behaviors, or, more effectively, rewards for good behavior.

The best results will come about by focusing on one behavior at a time with a variety of methods used. For instance, if you want to start thinking more positively, start becoming aware of why negative thoughts rule your brain, and what situations led you to have that mindset. If possible, cut out sources that are reinforcing that negativity. After this, actively say positive things. Write gratitude lists, consume positive media, and surround yourself with positive people. Your brain may initially reject these new energies, so you will have to practice forms of letting go or learning to be uncomfortable until you achieve integrating the new behavior.

Your subconscious can actually change itself without your conscious input as well. For instance, dreams may change how you feel about people around you in your waking life. Stress experienced from the same source multiple times can make that stress become worse or turn into a self-limiting belief. This makes it especially important that you fill your subconscious mind with good things and learn how to reform its undesirable behaviors. The more your shadow or light form controls you, the more easily their individual energies will spread into the rest of your life. This is why a negative mindset tends to stay negative, and a positive mindset stays positive—these energies reinforce each other.

Entering Into Your Subconscious

The subconscious is more than just your instinctual behaviors, it is a vibrant world full of remarkable experiences, unique insights, creative inspiration, and a gateway to spiritual fulfillment. Visiting your subconscious world will allow you to tap into these as well as more directly influence subconscious behaviors. You can do so by:

- Exploring your imagination and dream world

- Noting the words, thoughts, movements, and energies you unconsciously use

- Immersing yourself into the arts and their metaphors

- Consuming certain magic potions

- Being in certain environments, especially in religious or spiritual spaces and nature

- Meditating

Of these, the dream world is the most direct view of your subconscious landscape. Repetitive dreams, especially nightmares, may be indicative of disturbances in the waking life. For example, dreams of being late or having an inability to gather all your possessions in time may be indicative of needing to declutter your life of objects or improve your transportation capabilities.

Wizards have many differing ideas about the symbolic meanings of the dream world. It may be helpful to consult with an expert on the contents of your dreams, but you can also analyze these images yourself and compare them to your waking life. What is their energetic quality? Do they seem to be pointing toward an unmet need? Perhaps you always dream about happily being around friends and family but lack this experience in real life, and so are being pushed toward forming meaningful relationships? Just like a sort of fortune made up of our personal experiences, dreams can be used to unravel hidden parts of ourselves. Not everyone remembers their dreams though. You can help promote dream memory by:

- Writing your dreams down whenever you remember them—leave a notepad and pen next to your bed.

- Not smoking cannabis or taking certain medications before bed.

- Thinking about wanting to dream before going to sleep.

- Affirming that you will remember your dreams in the morning.

- Not feeling rushed to get out of bed or to start thinking about anything when you wake up.

- Drinking or smoking a dream-promoting herb such as mullein or mugwort.

It is especially important to find the cause of nightmares because good dreams provide a deeper sense of rest and possible insight or healing. Often what you experience and think about during your waking hours seeps into your dreams. Try removing easily avoidable negative stimuli from your life such as horror movies and world news media. Working through other negative stimuli such as trauma or changing how you think and perceive the world around you may help as well.

To directly gain better control over your dreams and confront nightmares within the subconscious realm itself, consider taking a course in lucid dreaming. Lucid dreaming allows you to be partly conscious of your actions in dreams, controlling it in a similar way as you would with day dreaming in your imagination. Getting more or less sleep might also help. See RESTORING ENERGY under POWERING UP YOUR ENERGY for more about how to get better sleep.

• • •

Life Mapping

How do you allow your subconscious mind to speak? What types of dreams do you have and do any recur? What do you often imagine and daydream about? What types of emotions or objects come out in your art?

COPING WITH THE DARKNESS

*A*ll wizards will eventually confront and be submerged into the darkness, a term in magical language referring to things like anxiety, loneliness, sadness, depression, trauma, unhealthy thoughts, hatred, or destructive behaviors. Control over your conscious and subconscious magic while facing the darkness may become limited or nearly impossible, so it is essential to learn spells to protect yourself and ward off its attempts at taking over your life, ruining social connections, and making you feel terrible.

While the darkness is uncomfortable and difficult to contend with, it is not an evil thing. Beautiful insights and experiences can be found here and it is often an essential and natural part of personal growth. There are many wizards who become deeply wrapped up in the darkness and must learn ways of working alongside its ever-present voice. Others will be able to free themselves by making specific changes in their lives. The initial goal of coping with the darkness is having the ability to take care of your physical and emotional needs. This is an essential foundation that can then be built into finding contentment and happiness.

Most of the spells contained within this book can be used to defend yourself from various aspects of the darkness, especially with depressed feelings, anxiety, and trauma. In DESTRUCTIVE SPELLS WIZARDS ARE COMMONLY UNDER you learn about wizards who intentionally spread the darkness and MAGIC ALCHEMY covers how to fight against these wizards' nefarious actions.

Sources of the Darkness

While sources of the darkness are many, they all arise from "potentials" and "triggers." A darkness potential increases the likelihood of experiencing a form of darkness, but does not necessarily mean that you will. These can include:

- Forms of the darkness running in family and genetics

- Hormones and hormonal fluctuations

- Exposure to substances that cause genetic, hormonal, chemical, or neurological abnormalities

- Malnourishment

- The time of year one is born

- Not being properly nourished while in the womb or not being breastfed as a child

- Growing up in a negative space

- Experiencing traumatic events

- Growing up poor

- Cultural upbringing

- Discrimination

- Unmet social needs

- Communication styles

- Today's weather, or a particular type of weather over an extended period

- Thinking patterns such as obsessing over a negative thought or judging others

- Generally thinking too much and not doing enough activities that consume your mental energy

- Unmet basic needs

- Consuming foods or medications that cause inflammation in the body

- Things like low levels of serotonin, dopamine, and norepinephrine do not cause depression as is often cited, but may increase the potential of experiencing it

This list can be generalized into four broad categories: chronic genetic and chemical abnormalities, unmet needs, life events, and lifestyle choices. It may be difficult to discern which category or categories you fit into initially, but doing so is an essential starting point for coping with forms of the darkness.

A darkness trigger then, is what consumes a person with the darkness, often in the form of depression, sadness, anxiety, apathy, or panic. It may be difficult to directly associate one thing as a cause of your darkness, especially for triggers like addictions which initially feel good and then the next day may result in feeling anxious and sad. However, as you observe yourself over time you will begin to see patterns. Darkness triggers can include just about anything depending on the person, though some are more common than others. These include:

- Stressful or uncomfortable events like an argument or over-stimulating environment

- Not sleeping enough

- Thinking patterns such as obsessing over a negative thought or judging people around you

- Eating too much or not enough

- Sensitivity to certain foods

- The intake of alcohol and other substances

- A reminder of a traumatic event

- Viewing and/or listening to certain media, especially news stories, movies, books, music, etc. that contain violence, anger, and sadness

- Viewing and/or listening to media for an extended period of time

- Not enough social interaction

- Staying indoors

- Withdrawal symptoms from addictions to things such as food, media, drugs, medicines, and alcohol

- An inability to cope with societal pressures such as appearance, fitting in, gender expectations, and other cultural norms

- A darkness potential can act as a darkness trigger with factors like sleeplessness and malnourishment

Start taking into account how these various things influence you. In the next section we'll explore tactics for controlling the darkness in your life.

The Basics of Coping with the Darkness

The darkness can completely change your personality and perception of the world, and so when it does strike, it is important to be prepared with as many tools as possible for finding your way back to a state of contentment. There are four basic components of coping with most forms of the darkness:

1. Desiring change and contentment.

2. Becoming aware of your "potentials" and "triggers."

3. Creating a self-care schedule.

4. Reforming habits and other sources of suffering.

The goal with this road map is to create long-standing contentment and stability, rather than short-term happiness. Note that this will take time and a certain amount of trial and error. As personal discoveries are made you will have the choice of altering your lifestyle and ways of thinking. It might be frightening and difficult at times, but will pay off in the end by restoring a renewed sense of peace and purpose.

1) Desiring change and a more content life

A basic starting point to coping with the darkness is acknowledging that you are experiencing it and its impact on your ability to enjoy life. Perhaps you already know this, but the connection is not always easy, especially with the myths and stigmas surrounding some forms of darkness. It is also common to feel crummy but not acknowledge those feelings as signs of depression, anxiety, trauma, and so forth. In a lifetime, most everyone will experience some kind of darkness. Knowing what you're dealing with can allow you to better understand yourself and to reach a stronger sense of personal fulfillment.

Sometimes forms of the darkness will go away on their own, but when wanting to shorten the length of time you are consumed by its presence, you need to desire that change to happen. This is not always easy as motivational energy is sapped away while in the darkness.

Developing a set of activities or a routine that convinces your mind into wanting change and breaks apathetic behaviors is useful. Here is a list of things that I have used to fight apathy:

- Maintain a schedule with obligations that must be fulfilled. Even if you are feeling bad, being required to stay engaged with others and your hobbies will prevent apathy from sticking around for long.

- Avoid rationalizing feelings or creating self-fulfilling prophecies. For instance, instead of thinking of whether or not you'll enjoy an activity with friends, just go do it. You have no idea how you'll actually feel once you're there.

- Put yourself around people by going to a populated space. If you live with others, at the very least get out of your room and go to your living room or front porch. Seeing other people's interactions and emotions can be enlivening and you may even have a chance social encounter.

- Watch an emotionally stimulating movie with characters and situations that you can relate to. With movies you see people having fun, making friends, falling in love, competing, creating, winning, and generally doing amazing things that you could also be doing. Because movies have a complete story experienced in a single sitting, they seem to work better than television shows, video games, or fictitious books do. These other forms of media more often make my mood worse.

- Compete with yourself or others in an activity. It's much harder to be apathetic when you have a goal and are trying to succeed.

Making changes in your life can be excruciatingly difficult, especially ones embedded deeply in your habitual and subconscious mind. Often self-help guides make the unhealthy claim that it is all up to your personal willpower to change, but be realistic. You might rationally know you want to change but be strongly attached to something at an emotional level, or simply not have the energy or social confidence to try out new tactics. Instead, you can rely on others to push you to change, accepting that you don't personally have the power or talent to do it yourself. Have people supporting you and turn to a therapist, a doctor, a support group, your family, friends, or a community.

When you desire change, insights to solutions may be found in many places, including those that were previously meaningless to you. Books, memories, and words from friends hold more meaning in a place of inner turmoil. Reforming habits is also easier. The desire for change within a state of darkness is not just a time we desperately want to learn and grow; it is an ideal time to find and apply creative solutions to our difficulties.

2) Awareness of darkness potentials and triggers

Wizards may be predisposed to experiencing the darkness from birth or life circumstances and choices may bring it about. To become aware of your darkness potentials, explore what your childhood was like, difficult life experiences, and your nutrient intake. Find if you can correlate any of these to a change in your mood or behaviors that actively create negative feelings for you. Forms of the darkness caused by genetic abnormalities are difficult to uncover, but may be a likely culprit if other treatment methods do not respond well, or things like anxiety and depression runs in your family. For example, if you have never experienced depression until your 30s, 40s, or 50s, or if your depressive episodes occur cyclically on a daily or monthly basis, your hormones may be a primary factor in increasing the potential of your depression

For your darkness triggers, ask yourself what event or events triggered a negative mood. How did it make you feel? How did the mood end, or what alleviated your emotions? Form the triggers into a simple and accessible list of direct consequences that will help you acknowledge that there is a reason for the way you feel, and that it is not the norm. For example, "If I don't make plans with friends, I will end up staying home and feel alone and sad." Or, "If I don't communicate my frustrations and personal needs, I will obsess over them and feel angry for much longer." In this manner, you can focus on dealing with the cause rather than the negative thoughts and feelings created from falling into the darkness. It will also give you a road map of what you need to do in the future in order to either avoid the causes of your darkness, or transform those causes into something non-triggering.

As you discover the things that trigger forms of the darkness in your life, it is important to turn down, or suggest alternatives to, offers that involve these triggers. This may mean ending or not pursuing certain friendships. It may also mean having conversations about how you experience reality and have difficulty with certain movies, words, behaviors, actions, etc. You can say "I'd rather not watch that movie," "not today," "I want to leave," or "I dislike this, can we have quiet time instead?" Some triggers are deeply ingrained and may require reforming habits or processing and overcoming traumatic experiences.

3) Time for self-care and scheduling

Even if you always seem busy, you can still find the time to take care of yourself. If you can't read a book, listen to an audiobook. If you can't go to the gym, exercise while sitting down, or stretch while brushing your teeth. If you can't join a meditation group, meditate while eating food, or before going to sleep. In other words, combine self-care with the things you already do on a daily basis. You might also remove certain things or at least decrease the use of them in your life, such as using the internet and watching television. It all comes down to reforming how you think things should be done. Creating a schedule will also help you find that precious time.

A schedule acts as a reminder for what you need and want to do, and helps you find more time to enjoy life and practice self-care. The darkness often makes the desire to do anything plummet. Plans get canceled and work productivity slows. Daily routines may become unenjoyable. A schedule is an effective navigation tool for not losing your course and can take many forms, which you can read about in MAGICAL ACTIVITIES.

4) Reforming habits and autocasted magic

Habits of all kinds can be formed or deformed using the right techniques. Being actively immersed in an episode of darkness can make this difficult, and that is why it is so important to work on forming healthy habits whenever you are able to—cut out junk food, take up meditation or a physical activity, form new thinking patterns, and so on. Learn more about how to do this in CONTROLLING YOUR MAGIC.

Depression

The darkness which most frequently consumes a wizard's life in deeply negative ways is depression. Depression describes a diverse array of emotional and physical states that when combined together inhibits a wizard's ability to fully use magic. You might think of it as a magic cold in which the body is saying "slow down, there is something wrong that needs to be fixed." Symptoms can include:

- Feeling sad or empty.

- Feeling hopeless, irritable, anxious, or guilty.

- Loss of interest in your favorite activities.

- Feeling tired.

- Not being able to concentrate or remember details.

- Not being able to sleep, or sleeping too much.

- Overeating, or not wanting to eat at all.

- Aches or pains, headaches, cramps, or digestive problems.

- Thoughts of suicide or suicide attempts.

Everyone experiences depression uniquely and so the spells required to untangle its grasp on a person varies. Depression can also be accompanied by other chronic conditions such as anxiety, mania, schizophrenia, and bipolar. Talk to a doctor and psychiatrist to help sort out what your symptoms are indicating.

Trauma

Many cases of depression and other forms of darkness are caused by traumatic events. Trauma is emotional energy that becomes trapped in the body from a variety of difficult events. Without proper treatment, this emotional energy can continue to force the mind toward the darkness even decades after the initial incident. Traumatic events are often something people want to push out of their memory, but confronting these difficult experiences is another key to fully unlocking your magical potential.

Anyone can be traumatized, but it is most common in military personnel, victims of physical, mental, and sexual abuse, and survivors of severe injuries, violence, and car crashes. Intense breakups and the loss of loved ones can also result in trauma. These events form a trigger in which any stimuli that reminds the brain of previous trauma causes the fight or flight response to activate, creating an immediate sensation of danger, even in completely safe environments.

Trauma is completely treatable, but therapy is often necessary in order to help guide the brain away from irrational thoughts and provide tools for the traumatized to work with. If you cannot afford a therapist, there are a number of free online communities to help, books such as *Complex PTSD* by wizard Pete Walker, and affordable group trainings such as peer counseling and authentic relating circles that incorporate methods of trauma healing.

If therapy is an option for you, there are several types that may be used to stop symptoms of trauma and allow resumption of a normal life. Not everyone reacts the same and some therapists are less than helpful, so try several. Typically therapists will utilize a combination of techniques. Here are a few of them:

- Exposure Therapy: Exposes a person to stimuli related to their trauma, slowly convincing the mind that the trigger is safe. A person may be able to go through this process themselves by engaging in visualization practices, lucid dreaming, using virtual reality, watching videos, or otherwise slowly reintroducing a stimuli, however it is best to do this under the guidance of a therapist.

- Cognitive Behavioral Therapy (CBT): Uses a combination of tactics, including exposure therapy and fixing distorted beliefs by teaching people ways of replacing negative or incorrect thoughts with objective reasoning—for example turning "all dogs are bad" into "some dogs hurt people out of fear, and I can learn how to avoid that."

- Somatic Experiencing (SE): This type of therapy is based on the idea that trauma is energy that became trapped during a stressful event in particular body areas. SE explores an individual's present and past emotional states surrounding a traumatic experience and finds ways of helping them express that emotion in such a way that it is released. This can take the form of yelling, crying, dancing, or any directed energetic outburst after exposing the traumatic memory.

- Eye Movement Desensitization and Reprocessing (EMDR): Part of this surprisingly effective treatment simply has the patient follow a moving object with their eyes while vocally remembering details of their traumatic experience.

Medications such as anti-depressants and anti-anxiety drugs can also be used to relieve the symptoms of PTSD. Read more in MAGIC POTIONS.

How to Take Care of Yourself When Facing the Darkness

Read the list of triggers found at the beginning of this chapter to help figure out what the cause of your darkness is. Focus on addressing that trigger if possible and communicating with any necessary parties.

Here are some other options:

- Remove yourself from overstimulating environments.

- Create a safe environment by cleaning, putting on music, etc.

- Seek out help from someone such as a friend, therapist, or doctor. Everything is easier with reassurance and support from others.

- Write. Process the thoughts in your head, recall the best moments of your life, list what is going well for you, or figure out where you want to be and how to get there.

- Meditate and practice mindfulness. Don't allow repetitive negative thoughts to take over. Find contentment and goodness in the present moment.

- When negative self-talk begins, trust that what your brain says is untrue and disconnected from your rationality. Trust that the feelings will pass if you take care of yourself.

- Go to sleep.

- Play a game, read a book, or watch something that will occupy your mental energy.

- Admit yourself into a psychiatric ward and put yourself into the full care of medical professionals until you get better.

- Call a support line like the National Suicide Hotline at 1-800-273-8255.

If you have an episode of darkness caused by external factors, such as the death of a loved one or breaking up with your partner, there are a number of ways to cope with it. First realize that only time can heal some emotional injuries. The eventual goal is to keep living fully with activities, friends, and things that help maintain stability in your life. Until then have a safe space, whether it be a person or place, where you feel comfortable and unthreatened. Visit, call, or write a friend or family member to whom you can relate the experience. Hopefully they can reassure you and help calm some of your feelings.

If explaining your situation is difficult, ask for a hug or just to hang out and do something like watching a movie. This may be an easier means of understanding you are indeed loved and provide some calming energy. Another option is to use a non-destructive act that pulls your mind away from obsessive negative thoughts. These acts might include reading a book, working on art, socializing, going to sleep on time, meditating, watching television, listening to music, exercising, playing a game, or other methods outlined in this guide.

Sometimes bad feelings over an event won't go away until you genuinely force them to. Saying "this is the first day of my better life," or "it is silly that I'm still feeling like this, I'm moving on" can break you free of feelings you are holding onto. Other times feeling really awful will inspire you to create a new life. And yet other times you just need to wait until you run into the right person, make a new friend, or communicate to certain people about your grievances. Whatever you do though, try your best to keep pursuing your hobbies and social life—it will increase the likelihood of being knocked back onto stable ground.

When to Ask for Help

You might hesitate about approaching a stranger to discuss your emotional state, but it can be really helpful to see a medical professional to help you cope with forms of the darkness. At the very least they will give you new options to utilize as coping mechanisms. Only you can say when the time is right to see a doctor, therapist, herbalist, or other medical professional, but here are some ideas:

- You feel miserable all the time no matter what you do.

- You hurt yourself or have thoughts of hurting yourself or others.

- You have suicidal thoughts.

- You cannot handle taking care of yourself and you become unhealthy.

- You have repetitive negative thoughts.

- You have anxiety that interferes with your ability to live a healthy life or the life you want to live.

- You realize you need help.

- Your depression, anxiety, sadness, trauma, etc. interferes with basic social, professional, or interpersonal functioning on a day-to-day basis.

Transforming the Darkness of Others

Inevitably a friend, family member, or peer will become consumed by the darkness, most often by becoming sad or depressed. They may seem unfamiliar and act in a manner that is difficult for you. This is because their sense of reality has changed. It is difficult to help someone who doesn't want to be helped, but if they do, the end goal is to de-escalate extreme emotions, resume thinking within terms of their normal reality, and help them realize how to prevent a similar episode in the future. If you choose to help alchemize these feelings into more neutral or positive ones, there are a number of spells you can cast:

- Listen with empathy: Everyone loves being attentively listened to, and people going through hardship really appreciate being able to vent their frustrations.

- Offer compassion: Beyond empathy, compassion provides another level of emotional connection by offering your support—"That sounds really sad, what can I do to support you?" This offers help without being condescending, letting a loved one know that you care about them and respect their ability to take care of themselves. Unsolicited advice may come off as not really understanding a person's situation and can be emotionally insensitive.

- Help the person remove themselves from their thoughts with a positive experience.

- Ask leading questions to help a person make healthier decisions: Rather than providing unsolicited advice, asking questions that help a person self-reflect allows them to come to conclusions themselves.

- Help release trapped emotional energy: Many people do not allow their emotions to be released in healthy ways. See if you can help a person have an emotional release. You can help this pent-up energy move by offering an activity, ask probing questions that delve into the root of a problem, or ask the person where they feel the emotion and instruct them to focus on that spot.

- Stay in regular contact: Send a text, call, ask to hang out, share a funny meme, invite them out to eat, say nice things about them, and so on. People need people.

- Correct self-destructive, abusive, and distorted thinking: If you catch a person making false statements about themselves or those around them, call it out using your personal experience as a reference. If a person says "I'm no good" you might share "Hey, I hear that you're having a really hard time right now and just want to make sure you know that I really enjoy our time together."

- Ask before giving advice: Empowering a person to make changes on their own will lead to far more beneficial results. Sometimes people in difficult situations do not have the capacity to do a whole lot about their predicament, let alone openly listen. In fact, true healing is likely not possible unless a person wants change with their own mental energy. You can help provide the tools, but they must use them.

Make sure you are taking care of yourself in the process of transforming the darkness in another wizard, it is easy to burn out by absorbing too much darkness from another person's problems. You can learn many more techniques for helping those around you by studying Non-Violent Communication (see POWERING UP YOUR WORDS) and Peer Counseling (see POWERING UP YOUR MIND AND THOUGHTS).

If you believe that someone close to you is considering killing themselves, there are things you can do to help prevent it. While some people commit suicide with no warnings, those who are open about their feelings are in fact seeking help. Here are some actions you can take:

- Ask them directly if they are thinking of committing suicide, and have a conversation about it. If they want it, help connect them with professional mental support. A person depressed enough to commit suicide may not have the energy to seek help themselves.

- Express empathy for their feelings. Tell them that the feelings they are experiencing will pass with time.

- Call 1-800-273-8255 for someone to talk to through the National Suicide Hotline. They can offer confidential guidance, support, and help connect you with local resources.

- Even if your loved one asks for secrecy, and even if it is uncomfortable, tell people who are legally responsible for their well-being, such as their parents or a partner. A person with suicidal ideations needs support, not silence.

- Remember, there is always help and hope, and that every day is a new day with new possibilities.

- Do not allow a person to manipulate you into believing that you are the only reason why they are alive. Seek mental support yourself for help navigating the emotional difficulties of a friend's suicidal ideations or attempts.

For a more thorough guide on preventing suicide, see online resources like the Suicide Prevention Resource Center.

•　　•　　•

While forms of the darkness are natural to experience, many wizard clans around the world have cultures that make the conditions more likely to occur. These include things like individualism, unhealthy foods, greed, toxic communication styles, unequal rights, and many more that can be read about in DESTRUCTIVE SPELLS THAT WIZARDS ARE COMMONLY UNDER. All of these factors can be changed by introducing or undoing certain magic spells. If you would really like to see a difference in the world and decrease the possibility of any wizard being overcome with the darkness, consider becoming an alchemist of culture, or in common nomenclature, an activist. See MAGIC ALCHEMY for the specifics on how to alchemize destructive magic spells into healthier alternatives.

Motivating yourself, learning about potentials and triggers, reforming habits, and creating a schedule are the basic tools for applying self-care into your life. Note that not all of these techniques will work for everyone. Sometimes your culture, income, or personal interests may be in the way, but that is okay. What makes one person happy and content might do nothing for another, or even trigger depression or negative feelings in them, so it is your job to experiment. What activities, foods, medicines, environments, thoughts, and nutrients make you feel better? Which don't? Apply this knowledge to becoming a more fulfilled wizard.

•   •   •

Life Mapping

What are the potentials and triggers that cause you to feel depressed, anxious, sad, etc? What are your sources of depression and trauma? What makes you feel better? What sort of support could help you overcome the darkness?

QUESTS

Many wizards feel restless without a purpose or calling to pursue. Finding and completing quests which satisfy your passions will grant treasures of wizard equipment, increased magic potential, improved control over magic, awareness of new spells, and provide you with a sense of meaning. Common quests include school and education, reforming habits, traveling to a new place, winning a competition, finishing a creative work, starting a business, possessing something, or bettering your life.

All quests introduce risks and sacrifices, but it is in that vulnerability that the rewards become greatest. Lower level quests often must be completed before grander ones are accessible, but if you dedicate yourself to the long path, your options will be many. Even in cases where quests are forced upon a wizard, it is dedicating oneself to the goal that decides whether or not you will successfully complete the quest. You must take the first step and make the preparations or collect the tools to find triumph. Most quests will involve a journey, allies, obstacles, enemies, and treasure.

The Journey

A journey is the mental or physical movement in a quest. It has a beginning and ending, but may remain ongoing throughout a wizard's life or for many generations of a wizarding clan. The journey is rarely straightforward. It requires problem solving skills and figuring out what is the best way to obtain the treasure or goal.

Obstacles and Enemies

Various obstacles and enemies may impede a wizard along their journey. While these may take the form of other wizards, an established idea, monetary challenges, injuries, or a literal wall, the greatest obstacle is your own mind. Self-doubt, your ego refusing to let go of certain ideas, and forms of the darkness such as depression and trauma impede many wizards from completing a journey, sometimes even before the journey begins! That is why it is essential to practice good self-care and understand that change is always possible. Sometimes beating an enemy simply takes altering how you think. See COPING WITH THE DARKNESS and MAGIC ALCHEMY for more information.

Allies

Throughout your quest you will also encounter many allies. Allies are the greatest asset you have to completing your quest. Widening your network, seeking support from friends and family, gaining the companionship of a pet, or simply befriending yourself will lessen the work you must do alone to complete a given goal. See MAGICAL ALLIES to learn more.

Treasure

All quests grant a person treasure, though it need not be physical. It may be a mental reward that feels good or is important to you. Treasures can take the form of an adrenaline high, romance, monetary gain, education, a house, friendship, or memories of the quest itself and the ability to say that you completed it.

Choosing a Quest

There are an infinite number of quests to choose from, and the greatest ones you embark on will match with your personal needs and interests. Careful consideration should be given to long quests, such as careers and moving. Short quests on the other hand might be best sought out spontaneously, such as trying to cook a new dish or going to a party. You only have so much time in this life and therefore must be specific about the experiences and treasures you want. Of course, there is no way of knowing anything will go according to plan. There may be many treasures and experiences you never expected to find, or none at all. As you complete more quests, you will gain a better understanding of how future ones will be, but even then, there is great mystery in how any journey will unfold.

Even if you feel incapable of finishing a particular quest, it can still be quite beneficial to take it on. Doing so is one of the fastest ways of powering up your magic and learning how to claim victory in the future. Embarking on high level quests may even help you find influential forces that can help you grow even stronger.

•   •   •

Life Mapping

What quests are you on? What quests would you like to embark upon? What needs to happen for you to finish or start your quests?

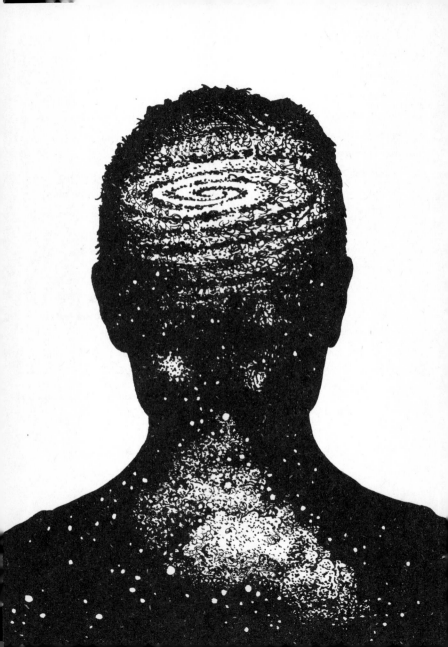

A WIZARD'S
HIGHEST FORM

*A*s wizards, each of us carry a complex combination of cultural beliefs and traditions that have formed throughout time. There is great wisdom and power available to us in this ancestral knowledge, that, if used mindfully, may help us unlock our highest forms of mind, body, and soul. This is one of the greatest quests that wizards may choose to embark on. Each wizard's highest form is unique, may change throughout a wizard's life, and can only be discovered through a wizard's personal inquiry into the realm of magic. There are so many different people with an infinite number of characteristics you could be, how do you choose which one is right? In order to get a better idea of what your highest form might look like, periodically ask yourself these seven questions:

- What have I always wanted to do?

- Who do I look up to?

- What experiences in my life have made me the happiest?

- What would I be doing if I didn't have to worry about money—Where would I want to be? What projects or experiences would I pursue?

- What am I capable of when I am absolutely confident in my words and actions?

- What am I passionate about to the core of my being—What makes my blood boil? What makes me swoon with love? What catches my attention without fail?

- What would I do if all my conflicts were settled, including the internal conflicts that fuel my negative feelings, ego, and need for approval?

When you answer these questions honestly, you open yourself up to seeing who you really want to be, regardless of what other wizards expect. Reaching this level of authenticity is rarely an easy road, but provides the ultimate sense of fulfillment when reached.

Keep in mind that knowing the true shape of your highest form requires a diverse set of experiences and may not be apparent until you explore more of life's rich offerings and great struggles. For most it is not something accomplished overnight, but rather over the course of years and decades of personal work. Your highest form may also only come out around particular people or in specific environments. Integrate what you can as you discover deeper layers of your truth, and know that this truth may transform over time.

While our highest form is more available to us than ever before, there are also more obstacles, destructive spells, and distractions to overcome. These can include things like addiction, media, depression, trauma, and the wizards who dictate your actions and thoughts in life. Diligence in transforming these obstacles with the spells outlined throughout this book is essential to seeing and obtaining your highest form and helping others obtain their own. We'll explore destructive spells in more depth later, but first it will be helpful to power up your magic with allies, activities, potions, and objects.

Life Mapping

Answer the questions outlined in this chapter to explore your highest form. It may be beneficial to return to these questions after completing your reading of *You Are A Great And Powerful Wizard*, or to create a life map as directed in the appendix, LIFE MAPPING. While only parts of your highest form may be available now, are there aspects of it you can integrate into your current situation or show around your friends? What is one simple change you can make that would bring you closer to the person you really want to be?

GROUP SPELLS AND MAGICAL ALLIES

izards are social creatures that have reached this current place in time because of collaboration. We need magical allies to help us grow greater magical potential and learn new spells. A group of people may gather together to collectively cast magic such as rituals, celebrations, love, potlucks, meditations, activist movements, and any other collaborative effort.

Group dynamics can be stressful, slow, and spendy. However, given the right spell, even if an individual wizard is hindered and cannot perform to their full capacity in a group, the right mix of people will typically be able to craft and cast that spell with a much greater power. Group magic can also be a lot of fun, fulfill social needs, and increase the availability of resources and opportunities. It is therefore beneficial for even shy and introverted wizards to figure out how to collectively cast spells.

Groups spells are most effective when cast with an established community or magical ally because your collective power usually strengthens as you build trust, create memories together, and weave various spells between each other. That said, collective magic may also be used by a random group of individuals with great impact.

Forming Magical Allies

A wizard's ability to network, find allies, form friendships, and emotionally connect with others greatly influences the wizard's ability to succeed. This is of course easier said than done. A connection with one of these allies may be an act of great vulnerability, and has the potential for creating something beneficial or devastating. As difficult as this could be, experiencing the negative and positive aspects of life will help you grow more powerful as a wizard.

As you develop passions and interests, finding like-minded wizards will become easier and easier. These connections provide support for when you're feeling down, share happy moments, and motivate you to do activities. Making magical allies is an art that anyone can become good at, but it takes practice and time.

Learn what works and what doesn't when communicating with a new wizard. Be sure you are consistent with social gatherings, or keep a ritual of contacting at least one person a day to make plans with or write to. Have activities that you regularly go to and can invite people to rather than just lounging around, or ask an acquaintance to teach you something they are passionate about.

Spend as much time socializing with people face-to-face as you can. While online interactions can lead to amazing connections, they can also increase feelings of disconnection and depression. It is healthier to use social media for organizing and learning about events in real life, rather than to maintain friendships. Face-to-face encounters also provide certainty for what people are saying with a full range of tone and nonverbal communication.

People tend to find it easy to talk about themselves, so be engaged in what the other person is saying and ask meaningful questions. Instead of "How are you?" or "What is the weather like these days?" try to be engaging and more specific:

- How did your _____ go?

- What was the best part of your day?

- Did you have any dreams last night? What about?

- Have you ever heard about _____?

- Have you ever read/watched/listened to _____?

- What do you think about _____?

- What's new and exciting for you lately?

- What's inspiring you right now?

- Where have you traveled?

- What is the weirdest thing you've ever seen?

- Tell me your life story.

- What was the best day of your life like?

- If you could live with just one memory for the rest of eternity, what would it be?

If making friends is difficult, you might want to consider how you are expressing yourself or how you are relating to others. Try your best to assert needs or boundaries for maintaining your personal well-being, even if that sometimes means ending a friendship. This process can be an opportunity for personal growth.

Know that friendship is two-sided, and both sides must provide something that the other needs. Both sides must also have the time to take on a new friend, though people can stay acquaintances for years before developing a close friendship. Close and long-term friendships tend to develop out of consistent contact on a daily or weekly basis over an extended period of time. People who travel or cannot consistently attend an event may have a harder time at making deeper friendships.

No matter what your problems are or what interests you have, someone will likely share them. It's just a matter of figuring out who! This begins with putting yourself out into the world and being willing to make mistakes. If you experience forms of darkness such as anxiety or depression, you may feel a strong desire to withdraw socially, but challenge yourself to seek out connection. My experience is that even if I don't want to socialize, I feel better if I do, even if it's just going on a walk around town or reading a book in a tea house. Embracing labels, such as poet, artist, gardener, entrepreneur, etc. can be useful for connecting with groups too.

While friends may be great at cheering you up while you are down, remember that suffering tends to create more suffering. Repetitively complaining or venting about the same thing is draining to others and is not a constructive outlet. If you have a lot of thoughts to process, seeking the aid of a therapist may be better than expending the energies of a friend. Unless your complaints are being used to work toward a healthy solution, consider transforming your social time used for venting into healthy outlets like exercising or cooking a nice meal. This is not to say that you should keep silent about your troubles, just be conscious that too much sharing of negative emotions may be difficult for others. Also, just because you want to say something does not mean that it has to be said. Walk in another person's shoes and give yourself time to calm emotions and process thoughts rationally; doing so will make your friends love you all the more.

Friendship is essential, but be wary of basing all your happiness on one person or one group of people. Doing so will eventually lead to a lot of pain because you will not have anyone if those social ties end. Beyond maintaining a diverse network of friends, be your own best friend. Take care of yourself and do things for yourself that make you happy. There is also the option of having an imaginary friend or being friends with non-living creatures such as a stuffed animal or piece of artwork. Having backups when friends bail, do unpleasant things, or turn toxic is important to recouping faster and warding off being upset.

Do you feel safe and comfortable around your friends? Can you be yourself? If a friendship is not working out, or consuming your time from making more meaningful friendships, it is okay to step back or end that friendship. This might involve a formal conversation, seeking out new friends, removing or unfollowing that person on social media, or holding a ritual to help let go and move forward.

Romantic Relationships

Friendship can also develop romantically into a relationship. This love is the most powerful of magic spells, but it can be quite complicated to cast and unwieldy to maintain (see LOVE MORE under POWERING UP YOUR ENERGY). A healthy romance involves communication, consent, and maintaining other friendships. Through this you are given purpose and a person to feel safe around, but these emotions often come in extremes too. You will almost definitely experience extreme happiness and sorrow at some point. Even with those extremes in mind, sharing love is one of the greatest spells to experience. Of course, you don't need to engage in a romantic relationship to express or feel love; that can be done through friendships, platonic touch (see POWERING UP YOUR BODY MOTIONS), caring for an animal companion, or a number of other possibilities. Romance, however, can be the deepest expression of love.

Getting into a romantic relationship varies a lot between wizard types and clans. You'll need to learn what a particular person is most likely needing to be receptive. When flirting with a stranger there are a few nearly universal tactics:

- Being safe and respectful: For instance, don't corner them, make sexual comments about their body, touch them, or say bad things about them if they turn you down or aren't interested.

- Ensuring that they aren't stuck with you: Say that you've only got a few minutes, or you haven't connected with them yet but was hoping to if it's alright with them.

- Seek consent for all touch: Light and non-sexual touch may be appropriate without verbal agreement for the duration of a second or so depending on the context, individual, and environment. Watch body language, if they withdraw or show displeasure don't do it again. Verbal consent should be sought for any touch more intimate than a hand on a shoulder including hugs, kisses, and anything sexual.

- Check in nonverbally: Are they laughing? Are they getting closer to you? Do they maintain eye contact and is that contact bright and cheerful? These things indicate that they're probably interested.

- Humor: People love to laugh, so make some jokes.

- Peacocking: Wear something eye-catching that gives a person an easy way to ask you a question or compliment you.

- Confidence: Be confident, but without expectations.

- Good questions and meaningful conversation: People love talking about themselves as well as the things they are passionate about. It's useful to have a wide breadth of knowledge for connecting with a person. If you're not great at back and forth banter, consider memorizing some topics of interest and questions, especially for when silences arise.

- Depending on how the first interaction goes you can ask your new acquaintance for their contact info, invite them to doing an activity you enjoy (typically best if it's public), or keep hanging out through the night (remember consent and ask for permission!).

With already established acquaintances and friends (see FORMING MAGICAL ALLIES), social proximity is important to successful flirting. In other words, put yourself around the person you're interested in by engaging in the same activities, attending events they invite you to, asking to hang out, or striking up conversations through text, phone, and social media conversations. Don't be rude or obsessive, but do note if they enjoy having you around or not. A potential romantic interest will often only give you so much time to make a move before they either think you want friendship or they find someone else, so make a decision. Notice if they are being receptive, making time for you, or attending events you invite them to.

Sometimes this social contact naturally flows into a romantic place with people getting physically and emotionally closer, but other times you need to announce it to your love interest in different ways. You can also remove some of the awkwardness by just saying that you'd like to take them to some one-on-one activity, but this isn't as straightforward and could still be seen as simply a friendly gesture. To be more clear, you might use a more direct method, such as:

- Formally ask them, "Can I take you out on a date?"

- Be honest and tell them, "Hey, I have a crush on you and was wondering about how you felt about me?"

- In intimate situations, let them know, "I really like you, find you attractive, and would love to make out with you right now." Or just, "can we cuddle?"

- Many people casually or indirectly talk about their relationship needs by telling a crush about previous relationships, general criteria they are looking for, or interest in having children. This method, though not direct, allows you both to learn more about each other and makes it clear you are both seeking a relationship.

- Show your interest in being intimate by throwing it into a list. For instance, "I realized the other week that five things keep me happy: music, good conversations with friends, cuddling, nature, and movies." It gives your crush an opportunity to make their own list or reciprocate by saying that they love cuddling too.

You do have to be forward with people about your own desires or interest in them, or lack of interest. Some people get a lot of attention whether they want it or not, while others have to make the forward advances, which often leads to a lot of desperate advances and unwanted attention. This is a common and unhealthy dynamic, especially based on how attractive a person's body type and fashion choices are deemed by a certain culture.

Relationships are much more likely to succeed if a couple is absolutely stoked about each other from the beginning. It is easy to become caught up in the initial excitement of a new person, but if there are any red flags or you're saying "I like them but . . . " it may be better to hold off for other more compatible wizards. That said, relationships will always require some sacrifices on your part and your partner's to make everything work out. It may take several months of learning about each other and trying different things before you successfully mesh together.

As you date more people, you will gain a better idea of who your ideal match is and what factors you need to personally work on to obtain such a person. Get clear about what you are and what you are not willing to give up in a relationship. No one is perfect, including you. Maybe there is a theme in your relationships ending. You will only learn through the course of making yourself available to date.

While in a relationship, it can be useful to note each other's love languages. A love language is a person's preferred way of being shown affection to and helps build trust. It is beneficial if a couple shares the same love language, or at least is open to providing the ones that their partner enjoys. It can also be important to note if you or your partner has a dislike of certain love languages. According to wizard Gary Chapman, there are five, including:

- Receiving gifts like flowers or being taken out to dinner.

- Spending quality time together, such as by having emotional conversations, supporting each other, or just having a one-on-one activity that creates a happy memory.

- Words of affirmation such as "you're such a great partner" or "I'm here for you because I love you."

- Acts of service like helping your partner study or run errands.

- Physical touch such as cuddling, sex, and holding hands.

Once you establish a relationship, be wary of spending all your time with a partner. Doing so may make the relationship unhealthy. Continue to seek out new friends and spend time with old ones. If a partner is toxic or abusive in any way, it is not a healthy relationship and should be changed or ended. Even if breakups are hard, there are many other people to fall in love with, and being your own stable person is most important.

Most wizards will go through breakups as they and their partner change or find incompatibilities with each other. These can be emotionally exhausting and difficult, especially when dealing with unhealthy relationships or situations where either person doesn't have a good support network. Look for warning signs early and seek relationship counseling if possible. After a breakup, engage in lots of social activities and start meeting new people. If you can swing it, make out with a few people, find a new crush, snuggle with a friend, or sleep with someone for a night; this will help remind you that physical touch is widely available and other options exist. Since you shared something special with your ex-lover, hopefully you can turn it into a friendship, but this may require months to years apart for each person to re-establish healthy connections without the relationship.

One useful technique for maintaining stability is to get into a relationship with yourself. Love yourself. Go out with yourself. Do things that make you feel fulfilled and good. Acknowledge when you aren't spending enough time with you.

Family

Family can be one of the strongest forms of community due to the deep bonds created. It can also be extremely difficult, destroy relationships, and traumatize family members. Starting a healthy family involves many important factors. These include parents' biological and relationship changes, how to raise a happy young wizard, support from other family and community, education styles, and how to maintain your personal mental health.

Emotional Changes

Becoming pregnant alters your hormones, which creates emotional changes even after giving birth. Some of these hormonal shifts increase your awareness and connection to raising a child, but can change other emotions and behaviors as well. After childbirth, some people experience postpartum depression. This type of depression can be dealt with by using certain magic potions and techniques, but is quite difficult especially while trying to care for a newborn. These hormonal shifts may also alter your partner's hormones.

Emotions can also arise from the major relationship changes that pregnancy and raising children bring into your life. These can include not having sex for extended periods of time, lacking personal freedom, ignoring self-care, not having quality time with your partner, and general stresses from the child's behaviors. Despite the struggles, raising children can provide a deep sense of fulfillment and emotional connection unlike any other.

Raising a Healthy Child

Healthy and happy children come from parents who are supportive and caring. Children raised by parents with addictions and traumas will pass on harmful characteristics, but of course, children can still thrive in difficult environments. When considering raising a child, answer these questions:

- Why are you having children and is that reason going to be healthy for your children?

- Are you ready for children financially, mentally, and physically?

- Do you feel emotionally capable of being compassionate and loving with the added stress?

- Do you have a supportive community who can help you through the process?

- Do you know what to expect and how to nourish your child?

- Almost anyone can have children, and those children can survive into old age, but are those children going to be happy and enjoy life?

As was mentioned in TYPES OF WIZARDS, babies raised on breast milk develop healthier brains. Anything consumed, will be present in that milk, so be careful with what you are personally consuming.

While babies cannot use words to communicate, they can use sounds and non-verbal cues. The sooner you learn this language, the easier it will be to understand your child's needs. You can teach babies sign language to clarify what they are needing. Reading to them will also help, and is a great activity to share at any age.

Babies benefit from as much loving touch as possible. Holding, cuddling, and sleeping with your baby greatly helps with their brain development. Equally important is surrounding your child with positive and loving energy. Smiling and saying kind things to them, even if they cannot speak yet, fills them with trust and safety.

Treating your child with respect is important. Let them have some choice in matters. Allow them to figure things out on their own, or talk them through an activity instead of doing it for them. Converse with them about why they think or want something. Be curious and supportive. When you cannot give them their way, use clear communication that expresses your emotions and needs kindly. By doing so you allow children to practice compassion and empathy while also showing respect for their desires.

As young children have yet to fully develop their rational brain, you may have to give them a short while to change moods or become distracted by something else. Be patient and empathetic. You have largely learned how to control your emotions, but the world of a child is wrapped up in this moment. It is beneficial to teach a child how to state the reasoning behind their desire. For instance, instead of "I want to go," it could be, "I'm feeling tired and want to lay down" or "I want to catch up with my friends." Promoting this type of language will help you be more empathetic and kind. Again, be curious and ask them!

Another form of respect is giving children tasks to help you with. The teamwork in cooking, cleaning, and running errands together makes them feel important and teaches them necessary skills. Reward them with a compliment or something desirable. Generally you want to use positive reinforcement rather than negative reinforcement. The former gives a goal to strive for, whereas the latter does not provide an alternative, just a negative sensation.

All minds benefit from environments full of nature, art, friends, and soothing sounds. Have plants and give your children access to creative outlets like paint and musical instruments. While quiet spaces are important to have, so is a social atmosphere. Be sure your children are going to playgrounds, join you out in the bigger world, and have playdates with other small wizards. That being said, some children are introverts or sensitive to the world around them, so be mindful of forcing too much energy on them.

In part due to their emotional nature, children can begin forming addictions to things they really like and usually do not have the foresight that it might be harmful. Children do need a good amount of freedom to discover and learn about the world on their own, but some healthy guidance is essential as well. Just explain to them why you're limiting certain things.

While all these points are great in an ideal system, we do not live in a perfect world and there are many toxic aspects to our cultures forced upon us by the wizards in control. Nonetheless, giving a child as good of a life as you can will still allow them to develop into a wonderful adult. We live in complicated and confusing times, but humans are strong and resilient. Do what you can, and hopefully supportive allies can help with the rest.

Parenting allies help lift some of the burden of raising a child, as it can be profoundly difficult to do alone. Seek support from your communities and social services. You can read about how the nuclear family structure may not give you or your children the support they need in THE NUCLEAR FAMILY under DESTRUCTIVE SPELLS THAT WIZARDS ARE COMMONLY UNDER.

While public school often makes it easier for parents to have time for work and some free time away from their children, it is not necessarily the best option for all children. There are many alternative education styles which you can read about in SCHOOL under DESTRUCTIVE SPELLS THAT WIZARDS ARE COMMONLY UNDER. As children interact with more people, especially in a school setting, they will begin to develop a mixture of ideas separate from your own. This can be difficult, especially as your child develops behaviors you might disapprove of. However, the same applies even as they develop their own unique identity—give them love, positive support, and communicate your needs in healthy ways.

Maintaining Your Mental Health

As previously mentioned, giving birth and raising children can be incredibly challenging for parents. However, finding ways to maintain your mental health will not only help you feel better, it's also healthy for your children. You can use the techniques found in COPING WITH THE DARKNESS. Also consider taking time for yourself and being open and honest with your partner and children about how you're doing and asking for their support.

Familiars

Pets such as cats and dogs magically bolster your abilities by providing comfort and support. They help with one's social life because they make fairly forgiving friends and are easy to get along with. That is, so long as you take care of them properly. They can also help one learn about compassionate behavior, an essential skill with human friends. Read more about these non-human friends in FAMILIARS under POWERING UP YOUR BODY MOTIONS.

Communities

While friendships and romances will bolster your magical abilities and strengthen your mental fortitude, a community you resonate with will advance your powers as a wizard to the highest of levels. These groups can form unintentionally with no one calling themselves a community and gathering without particular rules about membership. There can also be a formal structure with a specific mission statement and guidelines to determine who is and is not a member. Belonging to a community takes a lot of pressure off of meeting people, makes finding social events easier, lowers individual expenses, gives a lot of meaning to one's life, and generally increases a person's safety, well-being, and opportunities through an expanded social network.

Non-human communities are also crucial and make up ecosystems which help maintain magical environments and the building blocks to life. These can include a herd of animals, a pile of rocks, a group of clouds, a forest, an arrangement of atoms, or even human compositions such as a piece of music, or repeated architectural elements.

Another way of thinking of a community is as a living organism in and of itself. Just as a vast community of cells and bacteria comprise human beings, so do humans comprise a greater entity through groups, cities, states, nations, and with animals, plants, the Earth, the solar system, our galaxy, and even the entirety of the universe. These various organisms carry unique characteristics and are able to cast different types of spells than any individual component that they are made of. All wizard-formed organisms may also contain their own highest forms of being. Thinking of communities in this way is helpful in diagnosing when the greater organism is sick, or what spells it is unaware of that would help it become healthier or more powerful.

It is also beneficial in thinking that some individual parts within an organism can simultaneously be essential, helpful, and destructive to the whole entity. When you perform your role within the macrocosm of an organism you consist of, you feel a sense of purpose fulfilled and a great surge of power. With all this in mind, it is essential to ensure the health and well-being of all sorts of communities, because they are part of the greater organisms you make up and are influencing you in significant ways.

Starting a Community

Starting a wizarding community isn't too difficult, and you are likely already a part of at least one, but in order to create something phenomenal that maximizes everyone's magical energies and wellness, there are some important guidelines to be aware of. In order to start a community:

- Create a mission statement or general goals you want to accomplish with your group.

- Get the word out to attract potential members with fliers, newspaper ads, word of mouth, a website, and social media. Gauge if each applicant is a good addition through interviews and specific membership criteria.

- Determine your policies including participation requirements and a method of terminating membership.

- Determine meeting times or what sort of regular activities you will gather around.

- Decide how you communicate, settle conflicts, and make decisions.

- Decide how you will vote on decisions, whether requiring everyone to agree in a consensus format, majority rule, or some other style.

The strongest communities will integrate a number of factors into their interpersonal dynamics (*Wright 2004*). These include:

- Sharing a common goal and culture.

- Having fewer than 150 members (the Dunbar Number), but less than 50 is ideal.

- Ensuring members feel physically and emotionally safe.

- Each member feels that they belong and have their social needs met.

- All members participate in meaningful ways.

- Members abide by the community dynamics and rules, but also have the power to transform them.

- Members are rewarded for positively impacting the community.

Ideas for Growing a Community

Communities can take on many forms, but here are some possibilities for building your own today:

- Tear down your fence and share a yard with a neighbor, or build a tool sharing library.

- Put up art around your neighborhood, a community message board in your front yard so people can advertise their events, or a poetry sharing board.

- Host a potluck—any gathering will benefit by incorporating food.

- Hold an activity at your house such as playing board games, movie night, yoga, meditation, or a garage sale.

- Introduce yourself to everyone that lives on your city block and let them know the skills and resources you have to share. Offer to teach people what you know.

- Have a neighborhood party where you visit each neighbor's house one by one with a unique theme in each, or in your own house you can throw a 'room to room' party.

- Create a neighborhood tool share.

- Ask the community to pitch in for a collective fund for things in this list or public needs like fixing a road. Alternatively share bills such as internet and garbage collection.

- Advertise neighborhood councils to gather and pressure the city to do this or that thing you want to see happen, like petition for low-cost housing, or ask them to fund art projects.

- Create a business that people commonly express interest in.

- Colorfully paint fire hydrants, utility boxes, and city blocks. Plant fruit trees for the public.

- Ask stores or bars to host an event, or just show up and do it.

- Create and maintain community spaces such as grange halls and park blocks.

- Collectively rent a building and sell your services or wares or use it as a community space for all members to use.

- Start a group that plays kickball or catch at the park.

.   .   .

Life Mapping

Who are the friends and allies you can rely on? What can you do to let romance into your life? What communities do you belong to? What behaviors can you alter to enhance your connection to magical allies? What can you do to build the communities you wish existed in your area?

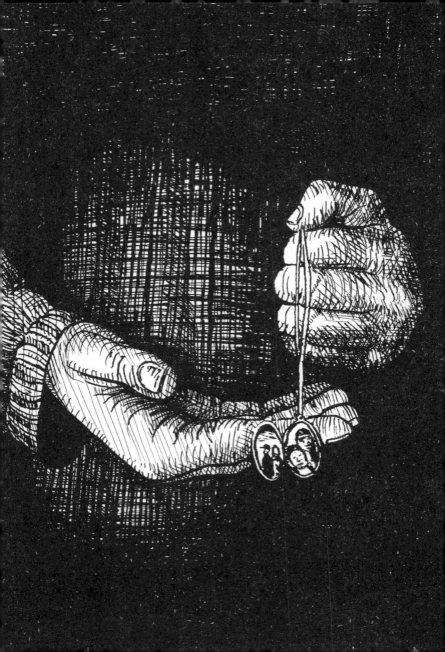

MAGICAL OBJECTS

ny object may be used to strengthen the magical powers of a wizard, especially when that object is within close enough proximity to be experienced by one of the senses. Sometimes simply knowing that an item exists or does not exist may also assist your abilities. For instance, you might draw power from knowing you possess an heirloom of your great grandmother's, or feel relieved you burned the letters given to you by an ex-lover.

Wizarding Equipment

For any given object you would like to use as part of your wizardly equipment, consider the materials, how they move with you, and most importantly, the spells the object casts on yourself and those around you. How do your possessions make you feel, move, think, and talk? Wizarding equipment includes those items you wear and your general fashion (see FASHION under POWERING UP YOUR BODY MOTIONS), as well as objects and tools used to channel magical energy, heighten one's magic potential, and improve the chances of success in casting a spell. These can include art, robots, musical instruments, a mode of transportation, and anything else that a wizard can utilize to improve their magical abilities. Be warned that simply being in possession of a piece of wizarding equipment will not necessarily help your spell casting success; you must know how to use it in conjunction with your inherent magical powers.

Grimoires

Grimoires, or magical spell books, offer great insights into the world of magic. These can include all written texts, but the most useful to directly improving your magical abilities may be found in those covering humanistic topics. While an article might be able to explain something to you quickly, a book can delve into the full breadth of a topic in a memorable way and illuminate areas that shorter pieces often leave out. Different grimoires will impact you more intensely depending on your personality and current state of mind. Don't be afraid to ask the people in your life or reference material online.

Art

Art, in its simplest definition, is a form of expression but it can also manifest in the process by which something is made. When you are fully immersed in art, the brain opens itself in peculiar ways. It is a doorway into your spiritual and subconscious self. Art isn't what it appears to be; a painting is much more than colors or an image on a canvas—it is an energetic representation of a person's collective energies including mental, physical, and spiritual. Read more in ARTS AND CRAFTS under MAGICAL ACTIVITIES and SPIRITUAL ENERGY under POWERING UP YOUR ENERGY.

Magic Within Your Environment

Magic is inherent within all spaces of the universe, and even in the undefined world outside of it. Individual magical objects combine into magical environments. Each space casts unique spells on you, which greatly influence the potency of your magic. You can add and subtract items from these spaces to create a desired effect. Consider the color, natural elements, amount of art, sounds, architecture, natural and artificial lighting, smells, temperature, and air flow. Together these create a space for magic to happen within.

Unfortunately there is a lot of thoughtless design in spaces made by wizards that diminishes magical capabilities. When designing a space, ask yourself—What problem is this solving? What sort of experience do I want people to have when interacting with this space? Many times the people creating spaces are simply cutting costs and corners. This means that many places do not empower magical abilities. Remember that when you are influencing the design of a space, you are impacting every single person who will be interacting with that space, including yourself.

If your personal environment doesn't nourish you, consider decorating or moving away before succumbing to the darkness—this includes work spaces, your home, your city, and even heavily logged mountainsides. Another option is to ensure you are regularly visiting environments with empowering magical energy such as natural areas, libraries, or art museums.

Imbuing Objects with Magical Power

There exist many spells which imbue an object with magical power. Any living or non-living object, as well as ideas and words, may be magically imbued. In order to experience these magical effects, wizards need a key to unlock the magic power contained within. The four most common ways of imbuing an object with magic power are with: **gift giving**, **experiences**, **inheritance**, and **focus**.

Gift giving

Gifting an object to another wizard immediately imbues that object with magic. Gifts that are thoughtfully selected and resonate with the desires of the receiving wizard will contain powerful magic. Selecting gifts without considering the type of wizard it is for may unintentionally imbue the gift with destructive magic. Consider what the receiving wizard wants and needs. What makes them smile and laugh? What aesthetic qualities do they appreciate? Could they use an experience? Have you said lately how much you appreciate them? Good gift givers are excellent at listening and observing. Write down ideas when they strike, otherwise the receiver will experience disappointment and at least some amount of awkwardness with what to do with unwanted gifts.

Experiences

Sharing experiences with objects, pets, and people imbues them with a variety of emotional associations. For better or worse, the more dynamic emotions experienced on the adventure, the stronger the spell cast on the objects with you. This type of magic is imbued especially well when regularly doing an activity, or when going on long travel adventures that take you out of your comfort zone.

Inheritance

Items inherited from deceased wizard family and friends imbue items with a different sort of magic than gifts do. The memories of the dead course through these objects, giving the holder a direct connection with the lived experiences of wizards long past. A lock of hair, a vase, ashes, jewelry, clothing, dishes, recipes, sayings, and more can be imbued with an energy of inheritance. In the case of antiques acquired from a random source, you do not have the key to access the magic previously imbued in the item. Even for items that you have some backstory for, the magic in these are much weaker than those connected to you by blood (see below, UNLOCKING THE POWER WITHIN).

Focus

Wizards may also imbue an object by focusing their magical energies upon it. This may be accomplished by an individual wizard or a clan of wizards by associating an object with an idea, thought, usage, or emotion. Many clans of wizards have unique ideas of the magic energies contained within various objects. Each of these unique ideas are equally true with the proper key to unlock the meaning that wizard clan holds as the basis of reality. It's unlikely you will ever fully be able to unlock the complete magic of another wizard clan's objects, but vaguely understanding what lies inside can be powerful in its own way.

Unlocking the Magic Within

If you are gifting a magically imbued item to another, tell them how to access the item's power by relating its history, usage, or your emotional connection to it. For instance, say how your parents used the item, or how you found it in your travels. These details act as keys to unlock the object's magic. This makes keys quite easy to lose, and it may be that an object's magical potency comes and goes as a person is able to conjure the key at varying times throughout their life. Various people may also have many different keys for the same object. This is especially the case for a person who creates an object versus someone who purchases or is gifted the object. For instance the engineers of a playground, compared to the children playing, compared to the adults looking over their children. Each sees the playground quite differently between the equipment's measurements, having fun, and worries of the children's safety on this or that contraption.

Even if you are not given the key, sometimes you will be able to unlock a portion of the magic within by looking deeply at an object and considering its history. This is notably easier with antiques and items that you find aesthetically beautiful. A useful starting point is researching when and where the object and its components were made, and then imagining the different people that have interacted with it.

Imbuing Positive Magic

The easiest way to instill an object with "positive" magic yourself is by gifting it to another wizard. This act expresses kindness and generosity, so when the receiver of the gift sees or thinks of the item, they will recall you and the joy experienced when receiving it. Gifts can also come from other life-forms and earth itself, such as if a bird drops a feather in front of you or you find a special stone.

You can also insert positive magic simply by thinking good thoughts about someone or something, or recalling fond memories with them. This can build over time or more immediately. For example, you might develop a deep connection with a guitar by singing songs on it for many years, or you could write a gratitude list about someone and recognize that you like them a lot.

Beyond individually imbuing magic, wizard clans can collectively do it as well. Take for instance the romantic nature of red roses, or the happiness many people get when they see a cat—these are imbued spells working their magic on you. Be warned though that destructive magic can strongly attach to any object without warning. Train in your wizardly practices to avoid these magical misfires by referring to POWERING UP YOUR MIND AND THOUGHTS and DESTRUCTIVE SPELLS THAT WIZARDS ARE

COMMONLY UNDER. If this sort of energy does attach onto yourself or your possessions, it may be important to your well-being to alter or be rid of it.

Removing Items Imbued with the Darkness

It is important to remove items from your life imbued with the darkness and destructive magic, otherwise they will constantly sap energy from you. What items cause you stress? Which do you associate with bad memories? What is holding you back in unhappy times of the past? Even if you do not see them, simply having items like these in your physical space and periodically remembering they exist can be draining. Consider ridding of or creating something new with these containers of darkness.

. . .

Life Mapping

What magical objects exist in your life? What objects could you imbue with magic? What magical objects would help you succeed in life?

MAGIC POTIONS

Sometimes you need a little help casting a magic spell. Magic potions include anything ingested or absorbed by the body. Magic potions work by influencing the chemicals throughout your body, especially those found within the brain. Potions therefore may influence your physical, mental, and spiritual well-being. If used properly magic potions may temporarily or permanently enhance your magical abilities. Misuse of magic potions, however, may lead to ill effects. Tread with caution! Always consult a doctor before taking any magic potion known to have potentially hazardous side-effects.

Not all potions work the same for everyone. Some people need a particular magic potion to function normally within a wizard clan due to being born with chemical or genetic abnormalities that prevent certain processes from happening naturally. People may also develop abnormalities during their lifetime. Usually you can influence these life-altering chemicals with potions and how you treat yourself through eating, exercising, sleeping, and taking supplements or medicines.

Many magic potions also interact with other magic potions, in both beneficial and negative ways. The effects of each potion may also change depending on a wizard's age. Believing something will help you can by itself slightly improve your symptoms, or in other words have a placebo effect. The combinations are endless and complicated, so do your research, consult a doctor, and listen to your body.

Food

Food potions are the most diversely creative of basic wizarding needs. This makes food an amazing thing to share, celebrate, derive joy from, and even find spiritual fulfillment in. Unfortunately, food can also be destructive to one's physical and mental health. Poor diet is the result of not consuming the right foods and consuming the wrong foods.

My personal journey with food has been long and difficult, but I've learned a lot and eventually found freedom from most symptoms I experienced. Many of the tips here are derived from what I have personally used to control various food addictions and pinpoint foods that were causing me unwanted trouble. Please understand that this will be unique to every individual, and what worked for me may be entirely different for you. Part of this journey has also been a personal acceptance of things that I could not or did not want to change, even if those things are deemed unhealthy by the "health" industry.

The "health" industry is full of deeply unhealthy thinking patterns that may increase negative feelings about yourself, especially if your body type or abilities are not capable of matching what the industry professes as ideal. Food should be fun. Much of diet culture plays on extremes and makes us fearful of eating certain things, so be careful of falling into the associated stress if you do start dieting. You may also have trouble having access to healthy alternatives due to living in an area lacking a proper grocery store, or certain items may be prohibitively expensive. That said, any body type can be healthy and feel good, and much of that has to do with checking in with what personally feels nourishing to you. You can also read more about accepting your body and ailments in ACCEPTING WHO YOU ARE under POWERING UP YOUR MIND AND THOUGHTS.

Changing your diet is entirely up to you, but if you are experiencing certain health conditions, would like to look different, want to live longer and avoid future health problems, or just generally don't feel good after consuming certain potions, you may want to experiment with what you are putting into your body. Depending on your body type, age, ethnicity, and lifestyle, you may need a slightly different diet than others, but there are general guidelines to healthy eating:

- Always stay hydrated. Try forming a habit of drinking water when you wake up, throughout the day, and whenever you start feeling hungry.

- Make time to have breakfast and a mid-morning snack, both of which have been shown to improve mood (*Smith, Andrew P. and Amanda Wilds 2009*).

- Consume a wide assortment of both cooked and raw whole foods with a variety of colors. If this is difficult to afford, try growing vegetables in a garden or pots.

- Eat regularly. Forgetting to eat or irregular eating may cause periods of low blood sugar, resulting in irritation, stress, and tiredness.

- Avoid heavily processed foods lacking in nutrients, such as chips and candy.

- Eat from local and organic farms you know are not using toxic pesticides and herbicides.

- Maintaining healthy gut bacteria by regularly consuming prebiotic supplements and probiotic foods such as yogurt and sauerkraut help reduce stress (*Gregoire 2015*).

- See a nutritionist, dietitian, or seek online guidance to help figure out if you're missing any essential nutrients or need help creating a wholesome diet.

- There is a lot of misinformation about diet so check multiple sources and keep biases from places such as for-profit businesses in mind.

- Many people cannot easily digest certain foods or have an allergic reaction to them in subtle to major ways such as an upset stomach, acne, constipation, fatigue, stress, anxiety, or even depression. These wizards will have to exclude particular foods from their diets, eat in smaller portions, or avoid combining different food groups (see a food combining chart online). Seek out a dietitian or naturopath to learn what you need for your conditions.

Exclusion Diets

If you suspect a food or substance is the culprit of any condition you are experiencing, you can try going on an exclusion diet. This means removing a common allergen and replacing it with a typically less allergenic substitute. Avoid consuming processed foods during this time because many are packaged in the same facility as, or contain derivatives of, a food you may be avoiding. After several weeks without the commonly allergenic food, note any changes you experienced and see how you react to eating the food again; if your symptoms are the same, your doctor may recommend repeating this process with another allergen. Alternatively you can get an allergen test, although results tend to be only roughly accurate and must be combined with an exclusion diet to be conclusive.

Inflammatory Substances

Certain medications and foods cause inflammation, which can increase the potential of experiencing a depressive episode, anxiety, and pain (*Kresser 2014*). Common inflammatory foods include oils high in omega-6 fatty acids, trans fats, saturated fat from meat and dairy, sugar, refined grains such as white bread and pasta, alcohol, and gluten (*Klein 2013*). After consuming these substances you might become more sensitive in various ways. These effects can last into the next day or even longer if you continue to consume inflammatory potions. There are many anti-inflammatory magic potions (*Kresser 2014; Siple*). Here are some common ones:

- Berries
- Onions
- Garlic

- Broccoli

- Apples

- Almonds

- Olive oil

- Turmeric or the extract curcumin (must be combined with pepperine, or black pepper)

- Antioxidant rich foods

- Foods with omega-3 fatty acids such as fish

- Drinking lots of water after consuming an inflammatory meal

Eating Intentionally

Some people experience difficulty with unintentional eating, such as overeating. Here are some things that worked for me in bringing more intention to eating and changing habits:

- Start the day off with fats and protein. Carbohydrates or sweets heighten food cravings.

- Brush your teeth half an hour after your first and last meals, this will wash flavors from your mouth that might create food cravings later. A clean mouth can make random snacking less desirable.

- Eat meals at scheduled times throughout the day. Check in with yourself about how hungry you actually are during these scheduled times, and adjust your portions accordingly.

- Regift or compost foods you are given but are trying to avoid.

- Fill a bowl or plate with as much food as you think you'll want to eat and still feel good afterward.

- Eat slowly, focusing wholly on the flavor and texture of the food as well as the feelings in your stomach. No talking or thoughts, just mindfully experiencing the sensations. Stop when you feel full.

- Join a support group where members help each other control their eating.

- Cook your own meals.

- Say a prayer or give thanks for the food you are eating before you eat it.

- Be sure that your hunger is not actually a sign of dehydration or malnutrition.

- Grow some of your own food to see how much work goes into its creation.

- Do work away from the kitchen or outside of the house. Store food in cabinets or in the fridge to keep it out of sight.

- If you eat as a result of stress, a habit cue, try forming a parallel habit of breathing deeply or some other activity that lowers your stress levels.

- Create rules for yourself such as: I am only allowed to eat out while with friends, I will only consume sweets on celebratory occasions, or I am allowed to treat myself once per week.

- Contrary to the idea that eating everything on your plate is saving food, overeating is actually another form of food waste. Save money and your stomach by refrigerating leftovers or turning them into compost.

- See HABITS AND AUTOCASTING MAGIC SPELLS under CONTROLLING YOUR MAGIC for more tips on controlling your behaviors.

Vitamins and Minerals

The vitamins and minerals contained within food potions help the body and brain function optimally. For instance, people diagnosed with severe depression often lack one or more of the following nutrients: fiber, omega-3 fatty acid, the B vitamins, vitamin C, calcium, magnesium, potassium, iron, phosphorus, zinc, vitamin D, and selenium. Nearly all of these vitamins and minerals are well established in maintaining healthy brain function.

A wholesome diet with lots of variety will get you most of the nutrients you need to be healthy, but how each individual's body processes it is complex, so deficiencies may still arise. Nutrients from fruits and vegetables are dependent upon the soil they are grown in. A deficiency in the soil means a deficiency in the food grown. If possible, get to know your local farmer and ask them how they grow your food.

Vitamins and minerals interact in complex ways with each other as well as other nutrients, genes, and chemicals, making nutrition a constantly evolving science with new breakthroughs. If you are experiencing an ailment that might be nutrient related, consider having a medical professional test your nutrient levels. The nutritionist may instruct you to supplement with a multivitamin or eat more of certain foods. Just be sure to do research on any supplement recommended.

Note that fortifying nutrients you are deficient in after a nutrient test may not be enough. Several genetic conditions and diseases cause malabsorption and prevent your body from optimal mental and physical health. Therefore a second nutrient test or genetic testing is necessary to know if these nutrients are being absorbed properly.

While every vitamin and mineral is important to wizardly health and has numerous intricacies, the one which most often causes people to fall into forms of the darkness is Vitamin D (*Crowther 2010, 1*). A person can become vitamin D deficient any time of the year by not getting enough direct sunlight, or by wearing too much sunscreen or clothing. Skin color also affects the body's uptake of vitamin D with lighter skinned people absorbing more. The Office of Dietary Supplements recommends exposure to the outside for 5-30 minutes at least twice per week to absorb enough of the nutrient when sunlight is available, and for people with darker skin to supplement that intake when there is little sunlight (*Dietary Supplement Fact Sheet: Vitamin D*). Vitamin D production from the sun's UVB radiation is most powerful in the summer during the hours of 10AM-3PM, but may be non-existent during the Winter months (*Holick 2004*). Vitamin D does store up in the body, so it is possible with enough sun exposure for it to last throughout the year, but especially if living above the 37th latitude, you may have to supplement or consume vitamin D rich foods.

Hormone Potions

All people experience hormonal fluctuations that regulate many functions and can heavily influence mood, though the science is not yet well understood. Levels of hormones, like testosterone and estrogen, even fluctuate throughout the day, as well as in monthly and seasonal cycles. For instance, estrogen may interact with other hormones to cause depressive moods during menstrual cycles, pregnancy, giving birth, and aging; and testosterone usually runs low in the evening, potentially reducing confidence and sex drive while increasing the potential for depressed feelings.

If you're experiencing severe mood swings or depression, or if your episodes occur cyclically, you may have hormonal depression. Talk to your doctor about having your hormone levels tested and possibly seeking hormone therapy. You may be instructed to consume or not consume certain foods high in substances that impact estrogen or testosterone levels, or you may be prescribed treatment which boosts your hormone levels.

Addictive Magic Potions

Many magic potions are addictive and can cause great suffering to the user when consumed in excess. People seek out temporary forms of happiness for the brain when they are unhappy, and these quick fixes tend to come in the form of potentially detrimental things like sweets, fried foods, drugs, and alcohol. Falling prey to these addictive substances is more likely for people living with stress and difficulties. The brain forms a strong positive association with these substances, and unless it keeps consuming them in higher and higher doses, a withdrawal effect will take place throwing the individual deeper into stress, anxiety, and depression.

There are no absolutes in terms of how any individual will react to a substance. Some of the items listed below can be quite beneficial for wizards in moderation. On the other hand, decreasing or removing any of these items might help a person's well-being. Be mindful of how each substance makes you feel after consuming them, or, consider excluding them from your diet for a period of time to ensure you do not build up an addiction.

Sugar and carbohydrates

Excess consumption of sugar increases the risk of cavities, anxiety, depression, type 2 diabetes, and many other health problems. It's also incredibly hard to quit. All carbohydrates convert into sugar and may cause similar effects, but replacing simple carbohydrates like white bread or sugar with eating whole grains and fruit can help.

Cigarettes

Cigarettes and nicotine are notorious for increasing the risk of many different kinds of cancer. Smoking has worked as a social and stress relieving aspect of people's lives, but you can find alternatives.

Caffeine

Many people consume various forms of caffeine, but long-term intake of the stimulant has been associated with a decrease in serotonin available for the body to use, even though serotonin levels increase (B.S. *Gupta* 1999, 21). For people taking pharmaceutical drugs, caffeine also interacts with some of the same receptors and may prevent the drugs from taking their full effect (*Carrillo* 2013, 127-153). Lastly, irregular consumption of caffeine can induce anxiety (*Childs E* 2008). Read about alternative ways to wake up in PHYSICAL ENERGY under POWERING UP YOUR ENERGY, or simply consume beverages with less caffeine such as green tea.

Alcohol

Although the center of a lot of people's social lives, alcohol consumption causes heightened levels of depression when the user sobers up (*Gail* 1987). Like most other mind-altering substances, consuming alcohol to avoid emotions and thoughts is not healthy. Drinking alcohol while taking certain medications is also not suggested because it can change how the medications interact with your mind and body.

While alcohol may feel beneficial for some people if used mindfully, there are other options to reap similar benefits. For instance, you can find alternatives to feeling comfort in social situations, such as with deep breathing, keeping busy preparing food, playing a game, or finding sober friends and communities that do not rely on substances to have fun. If you feel self-conscious about not drinking in social environments, you can ask bartenders for a fancy looking non-alcoholic drink, bring your own liquids to a party, or tell anyone who offers you a drink that "I've already got one."

If you want help with limiting or stopping your alcohol consumption, consider joining a supportive community. Being able to work together with others who relate to your suffering can be a powerful way to heal. The most popular program is *Alcoholics Anonymous*. Different A.A. chapters have varying levels of spirituality involved in them. For those who do not want that aspect of A.A., there is also *Secular Organizations for Sobriety* (S.O.S.), which shares a directory of alcohol and narcotics support groups that use a secular model of assistance. For family and friends of alcoholics, the support groups *Al-Anon* or *Alateen* may be able to help. If groups are not your thing, seeing a therapist is another helpful outlet.

Narcotics

Narcotics, also known as opioids, are substances that relieve pain. These potions help many people who otherwise would suffer from debilitating pain, but are also addictive and widely used improperly outside of medical supervision. Any narcotic, especially if used extensively or regularly, will create depressive feelings when coming down from its effects. Assistance for those dealing with addictions to narcotics can be found through *Narcotics Anonymous* or the previously mentioned *Secular Organizations for Sobriety*.

Air and Pollutant Potions

Some people experience chemical sensitivity and adverse effects from the toxins found in nearly all consumer products, the air, and in foods. Mold and dampness can cause depression as well, so if your home has these problems, consider using a dehumidifier or doing a deep clean (M Brown 2007). Keeping a window open to filter in fresh air will also help decrease a buildup of pollutants and disease-causing pathogens (Jessica Green 2011). Be conscientious of the toxins found within paint, shampoo, clothing, food, and construction materials like insulation.

Pharmaceutical and Herbal Magic Potions

Pharmaceutical and herbal medicines have a wide range of effects on wizards. If pregnant, check with your doctor before taking any medications or herbal supplements. This warning also applies to anyone with a medical condition or who is already consuming other magic potions. It is better to be safe than magically misfired!

Pharmaceutical potions

Pharmaceutical magic potions are usually a concentrated concoction of synthetic chemicals inspired by the desirable effects found in herbal potions. Even though they are relatively safe if used properly, the high concentration may create undesirable side-effects, so they must often be prescribed and monitored by a doctor. As everyone reacts a little differently, dosages may need to be adjusted, or you may need to take several of these magic potions together to acquire the desired effect.

If for any reason you need to switch or get off your medication(s), note that it may be emotionally difficult, so try to have a solid support network to help you through your transition. Talk to your doctor first to set up a schedule to slowly reduce your dosage; stopping your medication abruptly may result in symptoms of withdrawal such as heightened levels of depression.

Pharmaceutical treatments should generally be paired with other healing modalities as well. Many medications do not treat the root cause of your symptoms, but rather give you temporary relief in which your body can heal or you can function in a way that helps you live life better. Especially with the side-effects, expense, constant need to remember to take your medications, and long-term biochemical changes (most prevalent in younger wizards), pharmaceuticals are best used as a temporary solution when possible.

If a doctor only prescribes you with pharmaceuticals, inquire about lifestyle changes you could make or additional professionals you could see to better your symptoms. Be aware that you may need to perform research yourself beyond what your doctor tells you in order to find true healing. Alternatively, you may need to see multiple doctors—no one knows everything, and a different perspective can lend a great light to your experiences or offer novel approaches to your healing.

Herbal potions

Herbal magic potions are derived from natural sources. They can be quite potent and just as dangerous as pharmaceutical medicines, so similar precautions apply as stated above about pharmaceuticals. Herbs don't just have to be ingested via liquid or solid, they can also be used in aromatherapy and inhaled through the nose by smelling the raw potion or burning it.

Cannabis

Cannabis is a relatively safe substance with many beneficial abilities. In a comparison of studies research showed that for some people medical marijuana can reduce or stop symptoms of depression and anxiety, while for others, it can make depression worse (*procon.org 2005*). Many peer-reviewed studies associate heavy cannabis use with depression, anxiety, and increasing the chance of experiencing psychosis or schizophrenic episodes in people predisposed to these conditions (*Degenhardt 2003, 1493-1504; Cohen 2008, 357-368*). However, this may be dependent upon the strain of cannabis used, with strains containing little to no THC and higher amounts of CBD not creating the mental "high" effect commonly associated with cannabis. In stressful environments, THC can heavily alter brain chemistry in such a way that may cause more anxiety or depression, while CBD is known to be anti-psychotic and have a relaxing effect on body and mind.

Whatever form of cannabis you consume, these potions should be treated with care and only used from reliable sources. You can become addicted to cannabis just like any other substance. Avoid synthetic versions, also known as K2 or Spice, as they can be especially potent and dangerous to users. If you are new to cannabis, you might consider starting off with a lighter dosage or have the company of a buddy who can share the experience with you.

• • •

Life Mapping

What magic potions uplift you? Which are destructive to your well-being? How do the potions you consume help or hurt in achieving your goals? What could you ask your doctor or therapist about as it relates to the potions you consume?

MAGICAL ACTIVITIES

*A*ll activities are inherently magical by changing our reality and honing particular skills, but some are especially good at empowering wizardly pursuits. Taking part in activities and hobbies can help you connect socially and keep yourself in positive light. Activities that help others are especially fulfilling by occupying your time with making a difference and boosting self-esteem. Find what nourishes your well-being and increases your wizardly powers.

These activities can lead you to experiencing beauty, a euphoric feeling full of joy and meaning. Beauty is often found as part of being wholly present with your environment, or after a long journey or a great struggle. For instance, climbing to the top of a mountain, or falling in love with someone. While under special circumstances you may see your normal environment as beautiful, experiencing beauty often takes removing yourself from your daily routine and doing something that reconnects you with your body in a profound way. This may be more likely to happen when you are in an emotionally sensitive place, traveling, or are not occupied by thoughts.

The strongest forms of beauty are found in-person, because the sensations of the environment add to the experience. Going to an opera, for instance, will give you a much more intense emotion than listening to a recording. Beauty is not something that you can rationalize, so a simple description or an image in a magazine cannot do the original justice. In fact, you may be surprised by the intense emotions you experience when confronted by the original and true form you have otherwise only witnessed through second-hand sources.

Beauty is commonly found in pristine nature, art, stories, relationships, children, music, and succeeding at especially difficult tasks such as putting on an event or graduating from school. Certain magic potions, meditation, and a positive mindset also increase your capacity to experience beauty.

Building Systems for Success and Scheduling

Wizards who structure their short and long-term goals will be able to accomplish a great deal more by keeping on track and knowing how to handle different situations as they arise. This is especially important for people who are coping with the darkness and striving to reach their highest form. What types of activities, people, work, food, and experiences do you want to fill your life with?

The most common way to plot these out is in a schedule. This may take the form of a piece of paper, planner book, calendar, or phone application. Make sure to cover activities for your personal health first, and then include time for other things like volunteering, media entertainment, and hosting events. Scheduling too much time for others, or too much in general, might create stress and hardship and make you forget yourself. Once you've completed a task, it's especially nice to cross it off as an accomplishment. During difficult times you may want to schedule your entire day including waking up, eating, and so on. Allowing for some spontaneity is healthy, too.

Whenever you obtain a new planner, be sure to list out major events that you want to attend and any goals you want to meet. It's important to spend at least a few hours thinking about what kind of life experiences you want, as well as which ones you don't want. How can you show up for life in a happier and more fulfilling way? You may want to write out lists or create bubble diagrams of interconnected ideas, or rate each activity you currently participate in based on how healthy and emotionally fulfilling it is.

You can also create a reaction guide, which is a more generalized type of schedule in which you list out what you do in case of certain circumstances. For instance, you might create a reaction guide for when the darkness consumes you. What are effective coping strategies that will make you feel better and keep you out of trouble? Who can you speak with or call? What should you avoid doing? These lists must be put somewhere easily accessible so that you will read them when needed.

Beyond just planning for the future, you can also build skills to work more efficiently in the moment:

- Set aside an hour to schedule out your week.

- Make a plan before jumping into a project. What are all the tools, skills, and people you need to be successful?

- Think systematically about a project—can you speed up the process anywhere? Generally creating an assembly line in which you complete step one for all items requiring it before going to step two, etc. will create faster results than going through every step each time.

- Multi-task—bring food with you to work, meal prep, and accomplish tasks based on their proximity.

- Set alarms to take breaks, get back to work, and cut yourself off from a project for the day. Have a concrete start and end date for a project, and for large projects, completion dates on individual steps. This ensures you will not only begin working, but also avoid being a perfectionist and actually finish your project.

- Hire someone or find volunteers to help with your project or distracting tasks.

- Find a better paying job so you can work less and fill your schedule with more fun activities.

Deep Breathing

Slow, deep breathing (breathing into the abdomen or diaphragm) can provide a quick reduction in blood pressure and anxiety (*Cuda 2010*). If you are unfamiliar with deep breathing, slowly take a deep breath in through your nose. Your belly should expand before you exhale through either your nose or mouth. According to wizard Esther Sternberg, this intentional action prevents the production of stress hormones and in turn allows the body to calm itself. Reforming shallow breathing into a habit of deep breathing can even provide a long-term method of stress reduction. Even better is if you combine your deep breathing with meditation.

Meditation

Why can words, sounds, gestures, images, and other stimuli cause sadness, anger, anxiety, and other forms of the darkness? It is because these are magic spells that the mind fuels with thoughts and judgments and in turn obsesses over in a negative way. One method to gain control over this reaction, improve mood, and prevent depression is by using a mental exercise known as meditation (*Goolkasian et al. 2010*). There are many forms of meditation. The primary goal of most of these practices is to gain better control over the mind and body, but different styles uniquely accomplish different things.

One of the most popular forms of meditation is mindfulness meditation. With mindfulness you learn that there is an option to think or not to think, and that it is okay and often healthy not to. This is because the more you focus on a spell that has been cast on you, or that you are casting on yourself, the more influential and intense it becomes. Obsessing over negative or positive things can cause suffering. When someone trained in mindfulness becomes aware of those thought streams, they move their focus to the sensations of the present moment and are able to shut off negative spells infiltrating the mind. Mindfulness is one of the most powerful techniques for blocking destructive spells from influencing you.

Using mindfulness meditation makes it harder to be distracted by sadness or anxiety. At a basic level mindfulness provides us with a calming period where we can step back from extreme emotions prior to dealing with a situation with constructive rationality. Researchers have found that the act of regularly focusing on the present moment gradually "[increases] activity on the left side of the prefrontal cortex, which is associated with joyful and serene emotions" (*Harvard Mental Health Letter 2005*). Another benefit of practicing mindfulness is that it enhances our sensations. By removing judgments, getting out of our thoughts, and focusing wholly on what is, sights become more beautiful, smells are more aromatic, feelings are more sensual, food is more tasteful, and music sounds more pleasant. It is a sort of joyful perspective that, with practice, can be maintained indefinitely and transforms the whole world into a new oasis to experience.

Mindfulness is not an act of avoidance, but rather an awareness of what is healthy and what causes suffering while fully experiencing life. Some practice "living in the present moment" as ignoring the future and not making plans, but this is unhealthy and often harmful to others. A healthy practice of "living in the present moment" is being aware of your actions and where your thoughts are, whether in the past, present, or future, and how those thoughts and actions impact yourself and the world around you. Mindfulness can be used all the time, or simply when you notice a need to step back from your thoughts for a while. It is total focus and immersion into what is happening right now.

Mindfulness is a skill that takes time to develop. Joining a practice group will help, but there are many ways of practicing it anywhere and anytime alone. These include things like maintaining awareness of the sensations of your body, of an action you are performing, of a conversation, or of thoughts that arise, but the most common way of practicing mindfulness is following your breath. Your breath is always with you, and so it is a reliable focal point. The more you practice being aware of your breath, the easier being aware of other sensations and aspects of your life will be. Closing your eyes will help prevent distractions, but you can do this practice with your eyes open. Follow the air moving under your nostrils and down into your belly, and then follow it back out. Try doing this breathing awareness exercise for five to ten minutes daily as you first begin, and then challenge yourself to increase it to 20 or 30 minutes a day as you get better.

As you practice, thoughts and judgments of the past, present, and future may arise, but let them float away and return your focus to the sensations of the present moment found in your breathing. Keeping count of your breaths or saying "in" with each inward breath and "out" with each outward breath may help maintain your focus as well. Sometimes I note the emotions attached to a thought before returning to my breath by saying something like "I'm really excited about that," or "I have some anger built up around this person," just to acknowledge it and not ignore what I'm feeling in that present moment.

Another meditation option is to sit with an emotion and focus on it, fully experiencing the sensations it creates without thinking about it. Doing so will make the emotion go away much quicker because your thoughts are not fueling it with constant reminders. Once you have calmed down, use other techniques, such as writing, to process and deal with the situation.

One last technique is to train yourself to hear natural mindfulness bells. These stimuli remind you to focus on your breath and can include things like cars honking, a cell phone buzzing, or an angry person talking. Natural mindfulness bells are great because they rewrite how your brain processes an event by creating a new and positive habit for habit cues you normally find stressful or triggering (*Layton*). With enough practice it is possible to find calmness where once there was turmoil, just by breathing.

Prayer

Prayer is an individual act which can be used to seek forgiveness, give thanks, ask for support, or otherwise communicate with energies we perceive in the world. While often associated with a religious or spiritual lifestyle, prayer can also be practiced by a person with a secular worldview. Adding flourishes to what you pray to can also make the prayer more significant, for instance "great Sun which gives life to all beings on Earth, please protect me from the menaces of the darkness today." Prayer can take the form of talking to a person who isn't there, thinking out loud, or even a mantra meditation in which a positive or insightful phrase is said with each inward and outward breath.

Visualization

Visualization spells are a powerful imagination technique used by many wizards to experience uplifting emotions or to increase the likelihood of successfully casting difficult spells. Visualization works because, to the brain, there is little difference between what you experience through your imagination, dreams, subconscious, and shared reality, so spells may be cast in any plane of existence with similar effect. For instance you could conjure a person to speak empowering words to you or imagine a golden light to protect your heart from pain.

Visualization can also be used to practice casting spells. This is especially important if you only have one chance at success. Each visualization spell is unique to the caster and must be specifically designed for a desired outcome in the future. To use visualization in this way:

1) Choose a desired outcome.

2) Clearly imagine yourself performing all of the actions involved in reaching that outcome.

3) As you imagine this, make sure you are also imagining all of the associated sensations involved. Writing the visualization out or making a vision board with images will help—create the world surrounding your goal. What emotions will finishing that project create? What do you do about the obstacles that might obstruct your way? Imagine these things in vivid detail.

4) Repeating a visualization spell multiple times will increase the likelihood of success. Of course, a reasonable goal will also increase your chances of success. What are you capable of now? And with a little more practice, what could you be capable of?

5) Some forms of visualization can also be aided with a mirror. Mirrors help reflect what sort of movement-based spells you are casting in the world. Dressing up, making silly faces, and other visual experiments will expand your self-awareness and allow you to practice who you want to be seen as while acting out a visualization.

Rituals

The act of holding a ritual creates a space to deepen your emotions, commitments, or your desire to change. The components of the ritual are generally symbolic, but necessary to strengthen your feelings surrounding your goal. You have to believe in that goal to actualize it. In this space that you hold for yourself or with others, you might remind yourself what is important to you, move on from hurtful memories, end emotional ties to a friendship or relationship, or accept your transition into a new life.

Celebration

Celebration has always been a core aspect of the wizarding world. You can celebrate alone or with others. Rewarding yourself by celebrating the completion of a project or the passing of time is especially nice and gives the brain a rest after struggling through an exhausting period. You can even celebrate difficult changes in life that cause suffering. Rather than having these changes suddenly consume your life, meet them halfway and celebrate. Throw a party, go on a hike, hold a ritual, meditate, have a bonfire, scream at the top of a mountain, or anything that provides a release for you.

Gratitude and Volunteering

Gratitude is a spell that alleviates depression and improves happiness in oneself (*Seligman et al. 2005*). It can be expressed openly to others, silently to yourself, or directly to a particular object, idea, or part of nature. Gratitude spells commonly take the form of gifts, letters, donations, or a few kind words of appreciation for someone's existence. If you're becoming particularly ungrateful about life, start writing three things a day that you are grateful for and then read this list several times over. If you have trouble being grateful, you can alternatively write down everything that is going right in your life. Finding gratitude for people you have trouble being around is especially powerful in relieving negative feelings.

You can also show gratitude by volunteering with different groups. Partaking in volunteer or activist opportunities builds job skills, introduces you to new people, and provides a sense of fulfillment by working toward meaningful change. See ACTIVISM AND ALCHEMIZING THE MAGIC OF OTHER WIZARDS under MAGIC ALCHEMY.

Gardening and Farming

By gardening, you not only feel fulfilled through meeting the essential human need for food and nurturing other lifeforms, you also get exposure to the many health benefits of the outside world like fresh air and sunlight. Farming has the added benefit of usually being removed from city stresses, toxins, and pollutants.

Being in Nature

Being in nature has numerous benefits, including decreasing anxiety and depression (*Jordan 2015*). In fact, city wizards have a much greater chance of developing anxiety and mood disorders than country dwelling ones do. If you can cut out any thoughts of human civilization and be fully present with the sensations of the natural environment, you will feel your positive energies increase. This will naturally happen the longer you are out in undisturbed nature. Seeing massive forms of nature such as the ocean, a mountain, starry sky, or old growth forest can also help shrink your problems by reconnecting you with your mortality, the timescale of life, and the grand power of Earth.

Writing

Putting words to paper or computer are magic spells that can help process thoughts, find solutions to stressful situations, as well as record important life events. It is nice to be able to look back and know mental and physical accomplishments, or pick up on unhealthy situations and habits. Writing a thought or feeling also makes it stable and concrete, so that it does not have to be continuously repeated as it would be in the brain. In this way a thought can be developed rather than dwelled upon. Consider:

- Write a list of positive affirmations that you feel are true for yourself and put it on your wall to read each morning when you wake up.

- Pose questions to yourself or find thought provoking materials such as horoscopes, personality quizzes, books, or movies that create questions to explore your personality.

- Write about happy memories from your past, or about who, what, and where you want to be in the future. You can even keep a jar of these memories.

- Write about yourself from a third person perspective as if a good friend were talking about you.

- Name your fears and anxieties, their histories, and what value, or lack thereof, they have in your life.

- Write about common themes and behavioral patterns that may be causing you suffering.

- Write for others as a way of spreading your magic. Try blogs, zines, books, forums, and pamphlets.

Reading

Reading materials provide a lot of insight and opportunities for strengthening your magic. Ingesting these words can give you thought provoking talking points and teach you new spells. While you might believe that your ideas are set and that you know how the world works, you will surprise yourself with the many perspectives and experiences available to glean from. Remember, no one can learn everything, especially not on their own.

Art and Craft

Art is perhaps the most complex of languages, acting as a symbol filled with meaning and made by combining the spells of words, thoughts, motions, and energies together. Making art, or participating in art therapy sessions, can actually reduce depression, anxiety, and hopelessness (Judith 2009, 64-69; Hughes 2010). With art you actively use your mind and body to stay present and are also able to self-analyze in a sort of meditative way. You might also feel a self-esteem boost from having a physical relic of something you have accomplished, or by receiving positive feedback for your completed artwork (if you are willing to share it).

Art can take on many forms outside of traditional fine art. Why not play experimental music, make informational booklets, decorate your room, publish a community map, create a website, or build a strange object out of recycled objects? The sky's the limit, unless you build a space shuttle! When you make something yourself, you create a deeper connection and understanding with it in a way that is enlivening to see.

As an artist, most people are unaware of your inspiration, thoughts, emotions, and the general steps you took to create an artwork, but the process is just as important as the finished product. A good question to ask yourself is, "how can I create beauty beautifully?" In other words, what nourishes you and the world throughout your art making process?

Experiencing art can have a similar mental effect to making it. Art deepens our understanding of the world we live in by highlighting various aspects of it in an entertaining way. Artwork also connects us with others who have had similar experiences to our own without the need for speaking words. The impact of artwork is generally heightened by experiencing it in person. Just watch out for consuming art in unhealthy ways and disconnecting from reality. For more information see DESTRUCTIVE SPELLS THAT WIZARDS ARE COMMONLY UNDER.

The most powerful art is made through the collaboration of many creatives who use their magic to form an engaging experience for the viewer. Live music and arts festivals are especially potent by immersing all the senses into a new world. Your mind may initially feel overwhelmed or reject the new world it has been thrown into, but know that so long as you keep trying and remain open, you should be able to integrate into a new world of possibility within a few days. Because of this integration time, it can be helpful to arrive at festivals a few days early so you aren't acclimating during the actual event.

Sound and Music

So long as you enjoy it, any type of music will engage the pleasure centers of the brain and improve your mood (*Kemper 2005, 282-288*). Contrary to what some think, this can include music stereotypically viewed as sad or angry, such as death metal. These styles are often listened to as a symptom of depression rather than being the cause of a person's negative feelings (*Scheel 1999*).

Another option is natural sound. If you want to create a calming environment, listen to soothing recorded background sounds like rain, wind, and ocean waves. Better yet, get out into nature and listen to the real thing in the sounds of the river, ocean, wind, and woodland birds.

Adventures

Take a break from your day to day life and go on an adventure. This might be a celebration, an educational retreat, camping, hiking, visiting another country, or a quest (see QUESTS). Doing so lets you clear your head, meet new people, collect stories to tell, and discover new insights. Planned adventures bring a lot of exciting anticipation, whereas spontaneous ones lead to mysterious outcomes. The adrenaline rush that new experiences create also gives the body and mind a nice feeling. It is especially fun to connect with others who share your niche interests such as art shows or comic book fests. To connect with hobbyist groups look online and in the newspaper for conventions and meetings in your area, or start your own.

Massage and Acupuncture

Massage therapy has a number of therapeutic benefits including "reducing pain, increasing alertness, diminishing depression, and enhancing immune function" depending on what pressure points are worked on (Field, Tiffany M 1998). However, the massage must be given with at least moderate pressure for these benefits to take place (Field T 2010, 381-385). Light pressure will not work, so specify this to your massage therapist or buddy and get relaxed. You can also give yourself some of the same benefits by learning particular pressure points or using various massage tools such as a foam roller or trigger point massage cane. Certain forms of acupuncture, such as the NADA protocol that focuses on the ear's pressure points, can help the body in similar ways.

Sex and Masturbation

Sex and masturbation are motion spells that both have similar effects on the body by releasing serotonin and dopamine. Sex has the added perk of validating your personal qualities and bonding you more strongly to a person. On the other hand, sex comes with emotional and physical risks. Because of this, sex is not an ideal coping mechanism

Masturbation is a safer avenue to orgasmic pleasure than sex. Pornography can be part of a healthy masturbatory experience if consumed with full consciousness of what you are seeing. Mainstream porn has the tendency to promote unrealistic gender, relationship, and sexual roles and rarely represents how real sexual encounters occur.

Physical Activity

According to wizard Mike Evans, exercise decreases the severity of depression by thirty to fifty percent (*Evans 2011*). Thirty minutes to an hour a day of activities can do more than prevent depression, they reduce physical and mental ailments. The best mental health boost comes if you can work up a sweat. Change activities if you begin experiencing pain, but even if you feel fatigued all the time, exercise will only make your body stronger.

If you have trouble motivating yourself to exercise, get a friend to go with you or get a dog. If you have trouble finding time to exercise, do stretches while cooking, or lift weights watching television. Other energetic outbursts may be helpful as well such as singing, gardening, or making art.

•   •   •

Life Mapping

What magical activities do you currently employ in your life? What magical activities would you like to begin practicing and how would they benefit your life?

POWERING UP YOUR MIND AND THOUGHTS

Becoming aware of your thoughts is an important first step to transforming them into something more powerful. Having a strong mind and knowing how to cast certain thought spells is essential to becoming skilled at all other forms of magic, and is therefore the most important type to learn. Thought spells involve changing mental attitudes, unraveling mental distortions, and finding acceptance with oneself.

Many people go about everyday life thinking that if they just had one specific thing, a certain house, food, or more money, suddenly happiness would be theirs. But while magical objects can certainly help, they are not essential. Happiness and contentment can be found in any moment, even in great struggles. This is because a single frame of experience is wildly complex and has a million ways of being looked at—there is always something new to see inside yourself, others, and the environments which you reside in. Often what is blocking the way are simple thoughts.

Therapy

Everyone and everything you ever meet will be a teacher, whether they guide you toward or away from the thoughts, activities, and experiences bountiful in the world. There is knowledge in all interactions, but the most potent mentors include friends, family, therapists, spiritual and religious teachers, support groups, dreams, and horoscopes. Let's take a deeper look at each.

Professional therapists

Professional therapists are trained to help you get to the root of your psychological difficulties, analyze why you are experiencing mental suffering, confront those causes whether past or present, and teach you new spells to help strengthen your mind. Although often expensive, some therapists have sliding scale fees for low income wizards. Most insurance plans also cover therapy, or you can find cheap or free therapists through online resources. Every therapist is different, so if one doesn't work for you, another might. Don't be afraid of switching therapists! Interview a potential new therapist to make sure that you feel comfortable speaking with them and that they are knowledgeable in the areas you want to work on.

Unless you are having a crisis, it may be several weeks between beginning the process of searching for a therapist, working on your life with them, and seeing positive results. It is therefore beneficial to seek out a therapist while in a stable mood so you can immediately access help when in need. The paperwork you sign may revoke some of your confidentiality, but unless you are seriously considering suicide, going to harm someone, or a legal court asks for your files to be released, information you share with your therapist remains safe.

There are many different types of therapists, a number of which specialize in specific psychological conditions or relationships. Conduct research online or ask your doctor what type of therapy would best meet your needs.

Friends and family

Friends and family have a long history of seeing your emotions and decisions and are therefore great mirrors reflecting how your thoughts appear in the world as magic spells. These people have also greatly influenced your thoughts and might carry important clues into why you cast certain spells. Ask them about the past, what they thought about when you were in a particular phase of your life or general mood, or to give you feedback as a person.

Spiritual and religious teachers

Depending on your beliefs, some therapy is better found in spiritual and religious teachers. This therapy may take place one-on-one, in a congregation, in a group, in books or videos, or in a ceremony. If a particular teacher or belief doesn't seem to be resonating with your needs, there are many other spiritual and religious pathways to choose from.

Support groups

Each person in a support group can act as a reflection of yourself. Interacting with someone else who has been through the same experiences as you makes the act of speaking openly about your symptoms, past, or emotions much easier. A good support group incorporates fun activities, goal setting, positive affirmations, and mutual support. If a particular support group doesn't exist in your area you could start your own, or find ones that fit your needs online. Support groups can also take the form of multi-day retreats that focus on building personal skills, releasing pent up emotional energies, and creating new bonds.

Peer counseling

Peer counseling is a great way to take therapy into your own hands. Peer counseling training teaches you how to be counselor and counselee with two or more participants switching between the roles after a set amount of time. The training involves learning how to be an empathetic listener, release pent up emotional energy, and express needs in informal settings. The counselee is allowed to ask for anything (within reason) they might need to find peace, and the counselor helps them delve deeper into their emotions. This allows sessions to involve meditation, positive touch, crying, yelling, exercising, watching a show, or just sitting in silence. It can be remarkably powerful with the right pair or group of wizards and is much more affordable than traditional therapy.

Authentic relating games

Authentic relating is the practice of interacting with others using a combination of active listening, emotional presence, and a willingness to be vulnerable. While not all of the techniques can necessarily be applied directly to real world interactions, the games are amazingly effective at helping with personal growth, working through anxiety and trauma, and quickly developing close connections with others. A few of the practices include eye gazing, asking and answering questions, dancing freely, and role playing a variety of situations.

Dreams

Dreams can provide a great amount of healing and reflect our everyday world if we pay attention to this plane of subconscious existence. For instance, a dream can allow us to spend positive time with people we have yet to forgive in our waking life, or give us a peek at our highest form of being. See THE SUBCONSCIOUS to learn how to deal with nightmares and gain better control of your dreams.

Horoscopes

Horoscopes provide material to help deepen your understanding of yourself. Based on planetary alignment, position of the moon, where you were born, and your birth date, astrology is an alternative explanation of why things happen in your life. My favorites are *www.freewillastrology.com* and *www.chaninicholas.com*. You can learn about your personal astrological chart by going to *astro.cafeastrology.com*.

Gamify Your Life

Wizards love games because they are a low-risk way of accessing our brain's chemical reward system. You can even turn your own life or goals into games. Gamifying your life can improve motivation, lead to greater mental well-being, and help with forming habits and having fun. For instance, race against yourself to see how fast you can complete a task, try to improve your previous best, and give yourself rewards for big accomplishments.

Besides these examples, continue to challenge yourself and be the hero of your story. Can you grow personally through exploring certain thoughts? Can you practice a skill? Can you listen to an informational audio recording or listen to music and dance? Can you find humor in what you have normally seen as mundane? There are many options to make tasks more enjoyable, and all it takes is changing how you think about them. If you want to learn more, wizard Jane McGonigal writes about this extensively in her book *SuperBetter: A Revolutionary Approach to Getting Stronger, Happier, Braver and More Resilient— Powered by the Science of Games*.

Forgiveness

When we associate a person with a bad experience, we can choose to forgive or not forgive that person. Depending on what the other person did, you must decide whether or not forgiving them is the better option.

Would it cause you relief or result in more suffering? You may or may not announce that you are formally forgiving a person, but forgiveness is always a personal mental action. When forgiveness isn't an option, you can simply let go and move on from the situation, but that may mean ending the connection or moving away. If you want to forgive someone, you must do two things:

1) Desire to both forgive and continue creating new memories with the person in question, or at least focus on the positive memories you have with that person.

2) Stop thinking about what that person did or did not do.

This is much simpler if you can communicate with the person in question.

Communicating forgiveness

The easiest way to forgive someone is to communicate, preferably in person, whatever is frustrating you and ask for that person to change their behavior. If they value the connection, they will listen and heed your desires. When communicating your frustration, avoid using judgments and instead keep with observable facts and feelings. For instance: "When you broke my vase I felt really angry and am having trouble trusting you around my possessions." That will help a person feel much more open to communicating over saying something like, "you're a careless asshole." Read more about nonviolent communication in POWERING UP YOUR WORDS. If a person does not heed your desires, you may have to either accept a part of this person that you dislike, or cut them out of your life. In either case it is still healthy to let go of whatever action resulted in your feelings—otherwise you may negatively think over it for weeks or even years but create no change in what happened.

Forgiving yourself

While in many instances we need to forgive others, in some we need to forgive ourselves to relieve the self-criticism that emotionally weighs on us. Follow these steps:

1) Desire to forgive yourself.

2) Understand why what you did in the specific instance caused yourself or others suffering, and be willing to avoid recreating that series of events again.

3) Stop thinking about what you did or did not do.

4) Continue on with your life by participating in daily activities and spending time with people. It is most difficult to forgive yourself when you are isolated.

Helpful tips

1) Take time away from your source of frustration and form new memories with other people.

2) See a therapist and work through traumatic experiences surrounding a difficult to forgive person.

3) Don't wait around for the other person to apologize. Sometimes finding, naming, and apologizing for your own role in a conflict can greatly help soften a difficult conversation.

4) Create a gratitude list by writing down everything that you have appreciated about a person—does one bad experience have to destroy the connection you have? Read this many times over.

5) Forgive yourself and others as soon as possible. It may become more and more difficult to do so the longer you wait.

6) Understand that behind all anger is sadness. Instead of focusing on the anger, find out why you are sad.

7) If you can will yourself to dream or do visualization exercises about a person, working out emotions there can assist in the process of forgiveness.

8) Walk in their shoes—were they being intentionally hurtful? Did they have trauma from youth? Have empathy.

9) How many times do you forgive a person before you realize that they are not worth the pain? Is there a recurring pattern to what you need to forgive others for?

10) Just because something hurts or bothers you doesn't mean that you're right.

Remember You Have a Choice

Know that everything you do is optional. There are no rules that you must abide by for your life, only good directions to improve your well-being and chances of success in your wizardly pursuits. Once you realize this, change in even the most dire of circumstances will become more possible.

As you likely belong to a particular clan of wizards with set beliefs, it will be helpful to develop a dual mindset. In one, holding that everything is relative and malleable. In the other, that certain people, including yourself, believe exceedingly specific things about how this world works. The more flexible you are, the easier it becomes to maintain a fulfilled life, because you can grow when faced with adversity instead of becoming stuck.

Impermanence

The physical world is impermanent, constantly transitioning into new forms of existence. Objects break, people die, stars explode, and black holes devour matter. When time is removed from the equation, everything is essentially one—you, your friends, the ocean, trees, goldfish, grains of rice, meteorites, and all the rest of creation is constantly moving around between different bodies, taking on new magical potentiality.

While ideas, thoughts, and emotions are also impermanent, they can permanently exist over the course of your lifetime and even be carried on by other individuals or wizard clans for ages. Awareness of this can help you transform the components you find undesirable and foster permanence for those that you find useful. Learn more in MAGIC ALCHEMY.

Keeping in mind these two concepts of mental and physical impermanence, one may cast some truly potent spells. For instance, the impermanence of your physical reality gives you good reason to not be too worried about death or when your possessions break. At the same time, you realize that it's not the objects or the people that make you happy, but the emotional qualities and magic spells attached to them that create a special connection. It is therefore possible to maintain the emotional qualities even if those physical foundations are removed, for instance if someone dies or departs in some other way. If you lose an emotional quality because of losing a physical manifestation, know that the same emotions can be restored in time with other physical bodies.

That is why you can fall in love with multiple people, or have different best friends over the course of your lifetime.

Similarly, the concept of impermanence lends to realizing that things change, but can also change back. In other words, you can generally fix things if you screw up, just like with an eraser. It might be costly in time or money, but whether that be a friendship, a painting, or an emotion, there are ways to repair what has been done.

Accepting Who You Are

Mental suffering is often caused by health problems or feelings of inadequacy. It is important to realize that you are not alone in feeling judged or not good enough. Within the majority of wizard clans almost everyone grows up with self-doubt over their perceived imperfections. This is because the wizard clan's culture and media portrays images of perfection to strive for that are actually fictitious or unhealthy in nature.

There are times when having self-doubt or being judged make sense, and it makes sense to improve your life in such a way that you no longer are judged or have a need to feel self-doubt. Most of the time though, ignoring those stigmas makes more sense, especially when you have no control over the part of yourself in question, or when it is an unhealthy part to change. In these cases, practicing mindfulness meditation and doing things that boost your self-esteem can help alleviate negative feelings. A good starting point is to befriend people who do not judge you and who accept your personal qualities.

Another option is acknowledging that the majority of being able to do anything is simply believing in yourself and trying. Take small steps and do not expect perfection immediately. Lastly, clarify any fuzzy ideologies or habits you might have by identifying who you want to be perceived as and cutting out the actions that contradict that person.

Remember that you are only who you are in this present moment, and that every new moment you have an opportunity to change. Your past selves have helped develop you into who you are now, but those people are no longer you. Acknowledging in a room that it is your space and that nothing in that space from the past or future is happening can help get you out of your head. Take a moment to embrace and accept the person, the labels, and the interests you are now.

Remember also that your thoughts do not define you. It is not until you accept one of those thoughts as a belief that it becomes truly part of you. Until then, you can consider the truthfulness of the thought or throw it out. And furthermore, even if a thought has become a belief, it isn't set in stone and can be changed if you decide to alchemize it into a new form (see MAGIC ALCHEMY).

Sometimes accepting yourself can only come when you feel fully comfortable in your physical appearance. This might be easier around certain friends and groups, but for public settings you might consider dressing up, wearing a costume, or putting on a disguise. Makeup, glasses, a hat, or other slight changes can have a huge impact on your self-esteem. You can read more in FASHION under POWERING UP YOUR BODY MOTIONS.

Abundance Mentality and Fighting Regret

Another option of accepting who you are is to create an "abundance mentality" in your life. This works by replacing negative spells with more uplifting ones. Think about the positive things in your life instead of what you do not, or cannot have. Every moment, every interaction, and every new day is an opportunity to ask yourself, "how can I make this feel better?"

A lot of mental suffering stems from ingrained thinking patterns. While it is difficult to alter learned behaviors, it is possible, and well worth it. You have the most power over how you feel, as well as the ability to deflect or reduce what you don't want to feel. An abundance mentality gives you a tool in which to help do this. For instance, if you are anxious about going to visit someone, say aloud, "I am excited to know this person better" or "I'm joyful to have these new experiences today." If a friendship or romance doesn't work out, you could say "I am glad for this new-found time to develop myself and cultivate more relationships" or "I learned so much while with that person."

Thinking something will make you feel bad will most certainly make you feel bad, just as in a self-fulfilling prophecy. However, if you maintain an open mind to how an event will impact your emotions, or see the positive possibilities available to you through such an event, the negative feelings will remain for much less time or not be there at all. Do not confuse this with avoiding feelings—when regrets or tragedies do arise, you fully experience the pain they cause, but then move forward and use them as an opportunity to learn and grow.

By embracing an abundance mentality you become much more tolerant toward changes, whether people cancel plans on you or a difficult event happens in your life. Every moment is full of positive possibilities. See GRATITUDE AND VOLUNTEERING and WRITING under MAGICAL ACTIVITIES for more.

Fix Distorted Beliefs

You can alchemize thought spells that are not serving you well into more useful ones such as thoughts of confidence or thoughts of positivity. This spell is covered in MAGIC ALCHEMY as well as HABITS AND AUTOCASTING MAGIC SPELLS under CONTROLLING YOUR MAGIC.

Finding Purpose and Meaning in Life

Deciding on a specific purpose or passion can be a helpful grounding point to live life by, especially when you have a million options to choose from. Many pursue a purpose involving religion, spirituality, happiness, love, a hobby, friendship, family, or providing services. There is absolutely nothing wrong with living without an overall purpose or taking time to figure one or several out, so don't get discouraged. It is just helpful for some people.

Happiness will come when you focus on living your life fully without avoiding negative emotions and circumstances. Succeeding also creates happiness, but if you can be your genuine self while succeeding, you will also find a sense of meaning (*McGregor 1998*). You're not going to get a great emotional benefit out of succeeding in a job or relationship you find lackluster and limiting. This being the case, it is good to pursue hobbies and work you really enjoy and feel comfortable doing. What moves you?

Spiritual, Religious, and Philosophical Pathways

A spiritual or religious pathway offers many healthy ways of finding fulfillment and well-being. Community, meditation, prayer, and meaning are just a few of the things that some spiritual and religious groups provide. These groups tend to be deeply supportive and a great way to make social connections as well.

While any belief system can be healthy in its own way, one must be careful with ideologies that preach mentally unhealthy ideas such as hating a group of people or causing yourself harm. One must also be careful of personally using spiritual, religious, and philosophical beliefs as a means of justifying behaviors that cause themselves or others suffering. For instance, some people may use spirituality to reinforce a state of depression or abusive acts instead of seeking help. Read more about spirituality and religion in SPIRITUAL ENERGY under POWERING UP YOUR ENERGY.

Think Less, Do More

The modern era grants us an immensely large amount of time to think, but this also means we have more time to have negative thoughts. Be sure you balance the amount of time you are spending up in your head with activities. Remind yourself to think less and instead do more things which consume your mental energy. Or if you need to, meditate to shut off your thoughts altogether. You are not your thoughts, but you are your actions.

Memory

You can improve your memory by learning different memory techniques. Wizard Joshua Foer writes about this in his fascinating book, *Moonwalking With Einstein*. The main topic of discussion is the *memory palace*, in which memories are placed in a specific imagined environment, such as a house. Each memory is encoded as an imaginary object acting on another object, typically in a humorous, sexual, or strange way. The memory palace is a compelling concept because you could, for instance, build one in which you contain all of your happy memories, or all the answers to a quiz. There are also specific techniques for memorizing numbers and poetry better.

Understanding some basics about memory can help as well. Your short term memory can only store around seven items at a time (*McLeod 1998*). However, if information is grouped together, it is possible to recall more. This is partly why phone numbers are seven digits long, but also split into two parts. In order to store short term memories into your long term memory, two things can greatly help: first, repeating the short term information and second, sleeping and dreaming. That's why cramming right before a test is not the most effective method of study!

Genius, Creativity, Focus, and Motivation

Being a genius is not an inborn trait, but rather can be developed through how you use thought spells and spend your time. Of course, some forms of intellect are more difficult for people than others, but as mentioned in TYPES OF WIZARDS, there are many forms of intelligence, and each has its own class of genius. Genius is in fact simply a high level of creativity that generally benefits society in some way, so if you focus on building your creativity and apply it to the everyday needs of people, you can reach the title of genius.

The same techniques which help foster creativity also work to maintain motivation and focus. In essence, creativity requires a high level of motivation and focus, and so you can apply the tips below to just about any field you want to succeed in, from school and work to sports and romance. Some ways of fostering your inner genius, building motivation, staying focused, and bolstering your creativity include:

- Scheduling time to think and create. Practice is the only way to better yourself.

- Having a deadline such as with an event or pre-order shipment date. This may cause some healthy stress that inspires you to work harder and find sudden creative insights.

- Forcing yourself to make something each day or week, regardless of how terrible you think it is.

- Slowing down your expectations. Most creatives go through dozens of bad or unsuccessful ideas before they reach one successful concept to actualize. Nothing you do is a failure, it is all practice for something greater.

- Taking different classes requiring creativity such as painting, wood working, and writing.

- Experiencing new things and being vulnerable to experiencing uncomfortable situations.

- Being open to the possibility of weird ideas being true.

- Describing the world around you as metaphors.

- Becoming skilled in several different creative forms.

- Following successful creatives and learning about their daily lives. Wizard Chase Jarvis interviews creatives and unpacks their vast knowledge of success into actionable tips online.

- Creating for a particular audience. Genius is a social symbol, so if you know what people want, your work will be more likely to be considered great; but that doesn't mean you have to conform, creating your own unique style is important as well.

- Taking care of yourself so that your mental or physical health doesn't get in the way of your ability to create.

- If you have a great idea but feel overwhelmed by its immensity, breaking it up into smaller chunks or seek help.

- Creating small projects to balance with large ones so that you get the chemical rush of completing a project and remind yourself that it is possible.

- Putting yourself around sources of inspiration. Generally things that elicit strong emotional responses in you are great, even negative ones. If you have a negative response to something, it means that you can use your creativity to better that thing.

- Blocking and removing distractions such as food, the internet, family, or social outings.

- Learning when your creativity flows best. Perhaps it is right after you wake up, late at night, around crowds of people in a cafe, or while walking around in the world.

- Keeping a pen and paper with you at all times in order to write down sudden insights.

- Doing non-creative things and mindless work. If you always try to be creative, you may be missing out on opportunities for creativity to come to you. Either that, or overloading your brain so you burn out.

- Consuming creative media such as books, movies, fine art, and music.

- Seeking out and receiving feedback.

- Creating things continuously. Your creative outputs don't necessarily need to be good, but as you make more you will get better and create a style to be known for, so just start creating something.

- Marketing yourself. Even if what you create is good, it is unlikely to be seen by the masses initially. You need to also develop ways of becoming visible to people. Read more about business under MAGIC ALCHEMY.

Remember That Truth Is Relative

Every fact that you know is based on an assumption. All wizards are looking through lenses to acquire a version of truth—culture, television screens, glasses, eyeballs, and even our own biology dictate what we perceive as true. In other words, no one is ever actually looking at the true form of a thing, only preconceived notions of what it could be. Truth only exists when we create systems to contain it within.

The ideas we hold to be true within these systems are layered and changeable. What we now perceive as true we may one day view as false. We cannot see the layers of truth easily unless we have many experiences to draw from. What you hear from parents, scientists, religious leaders, dieticians, friends, and so on may one day transform into new truths. Just because someone says something is right, it is not necessarily so. The only way to know is to learn and experience for yourself what this moment's truth is for you.

Our prejudices, interests, beliefs, and so forth may all shift if we have experiences that take us out of our normal vantage point. Conversely, if your life becomes repetitive with no new experiences, or no enjoyment of new experiences, you will never witness the layers of your truth. Mind you, believing in certain truths will likely help you live longer and happier. Just know that everyone's truth is flexible.

•   •   •

Life Mapping

What are your mental strengths? Weaknesses? What thoughts consume your mind and how do those thoughts make you feel?

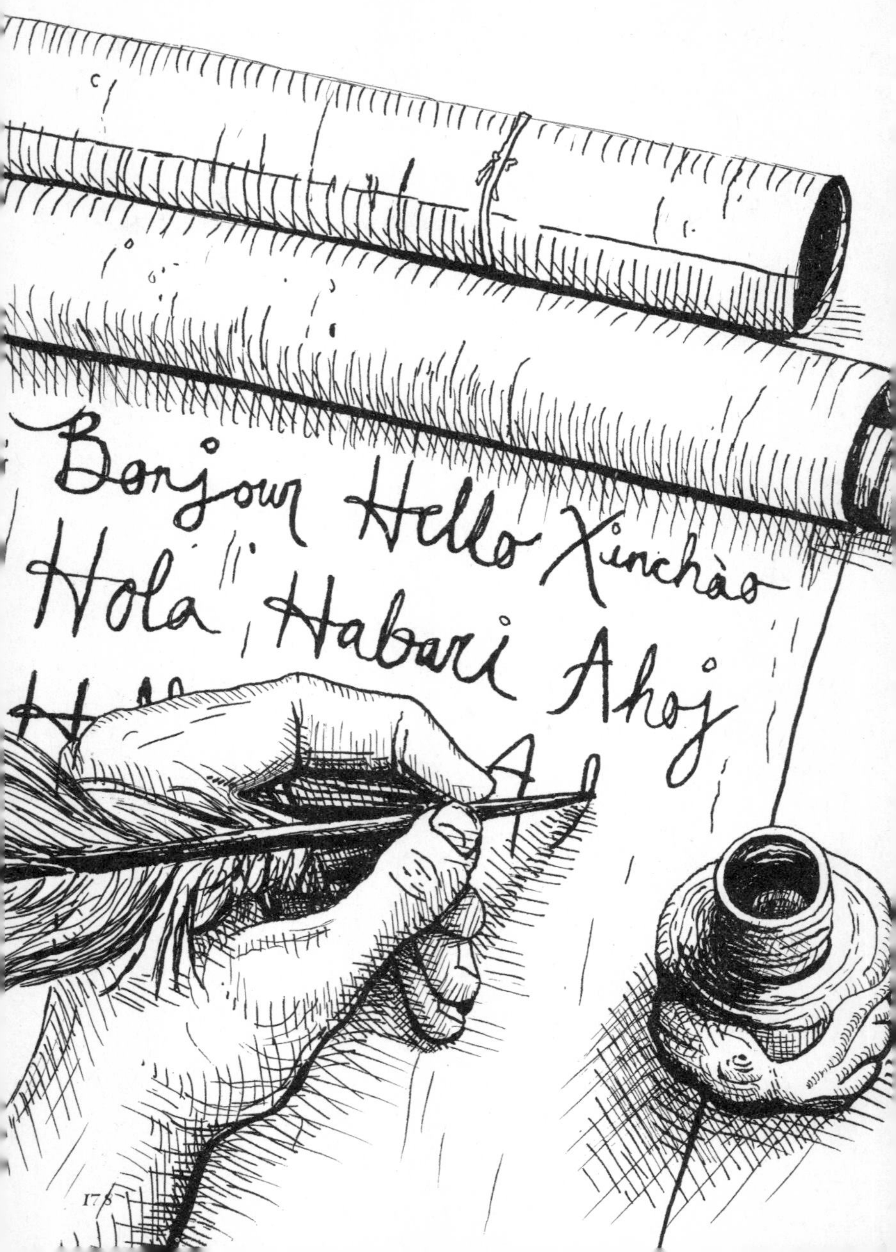
Bonjour Hello Xinchào
Hola Habari Ahoj

POWERING UP YOUR WORDS

*V*erbal magic uses words and tone of voice to communicate information or emotions with. Sometimes these spoken spells we use are not in line with how we want to be perceived, nor used in a way that attracts the friends and love we desire in our lives. Poor communication is the number one cause of conflict. One word, or the tone that it is delivered with, can completely alter the effect of a spell. It takes a great amount of mindfulness to determine why people treat you the way they do, but analyzing how you speak and use words may be a good place to start.

Do you want to sound more confident, swear less, say positive things more often, stop using words such as "umm" and "like," always have a joke handy as a conversation starter, or not be so argumentative? All of these are habits that take time to form or break. It may be helpful to practice alone to create new patterns of speech, and while in public, note when you use a speech pattern you dislike or that receives an undesired effect. See CONTROLLING YOUR MAGIC for the basics of transforming habits. Otherwise, this chapter covers some quick tips for powering up your verbal language.

Study

Improve your ability to use words by studying. You can read books of advanced levels, decode unfamiliar words, learn new languages, discover etymology and sociology, and find out various communication techniques like Nonviolent Communication. Knowing more words and how your language works will allow you to use a wider array of magic and reach a greater number of wizards. That said, the use of unique and rare words will reach a different and more particular audience than will easy and common words. Thus, you must not only learn the expanses of language, but also be able to gauge what aspects of language to use for a particular wizard or wizard clan.

Write

Writing is one form of magic casting usable on yourself and others. There are many things to write: keep a daily journal, write a letter, play with throwing traditional rules of language out in a poem, break reality a little, create bubble diagrams, and explore the many ways an emotion can be described or expressed. Read more in WRITING under MAGICAL ACTIVITIES.

Practice Speech

Verbal communication is the source of the most complicated and important spells. Learn it well by:

- Taking communication courses.

- Traveling and visiting other wizarding nations.

- Using a voice recorder to fine-tune your tone and pacing.

- Speaking to wizard clans other than your own.

- Learning what clicks with particular demographics of people and when to swear appropriately.

- Cutting out junk words like "umm."

- Singing and putting words to music.

- Trying to make new friends.

- Engaging in a romance.

- Discovering the nuances of speaking one-on-one with a person compared to addressing large groups.

Spells of Meaningful Connection

There are many ways to meaningfully connect with a person through language such as sharing interests, speaking confidently, and asking meaningful questions. These are covered extensively in GROUP SPELLS AND MAGICAL ALLIES and may lead to friendships, romances, allies, and community.

Written Versus Verbal Language

People "hear" written messages differently than the sender does. The writer perceives the message to have a specific emotional state but the reader usually fails transcribing the words into those emotions, and so misinterpretation may occur. Using written language also slows down the response time, may leave things unresolved, and makes it easier to dehumanize the other person. Therefore the written form tends to be a bad choice for serious or emotional conversations. If you have to use written communication:

- Instead of going into your emotions, say you'd like to arrange to speak in person or over the phone.

- Use empathy and consider the many possible explanations for what happened, instead of just the one where you are a victim. One technique for stepping into empathy is to note your own part in the disagreement, even if it's just that you haven't communicated sooner or that you feel upset.

- Take some space until you can rationalize the situation and step away from your emotions.

- Avoid violent forms of communication like name calling and belittling the recipient.

Communication Styles

There are many different ways that different wizarding clans communicate, but each individual can make a choice of whether or not to maintain their wizard clan's way of speaking. Becoming aware of how other cultures perceive your way of communicating and widening the ways in which you talk can greatly assist in your spell casting abilities. Below are some important notes on how wizards speak and alternative possibilities to consider.

Passive aggression

Passive aggressiveness generally takes the form of a person being angry or upset about something another person or group did, but says nothing about it. Often this anger will manifest in unhealthy ways. This is problematic because the other person or group did not necessarily do the upsetting thing on purpose. Since the "victim" does not communicate, no resolution can be reached and the perpetrators cannot clear up misunderstandings, accommodate the angry person's needs, or otherwise learn better ways of being.

Violent communication

Violent communication uses words which insult or demean a person, often with the intent of psychological harm. When you are verbally or physically attacked by someone, responding with violent communication may sometimes be beneficial. While violent communication is not ideal, remaining silent to injustices creates no change. Responding violently may be your only option when there is little time between standing up for yourself and never seeing a person again.

A violent rebuttal, more than anything, gives your ego a boost (though can also make you feel worse and put you in danger), and may also make a definitive statement that the thing said was problematic. However, this is dependent upon how the perpetrator communicates and thinks. Violent communication can actually reinforce negative feelings toward a person or group of people. Even more troublesome is that violent communication doesn't actually reveal the root problem of an issue, which is why Marshall Rosenberg developed Nonviolent Communication.

Nonviolent communication

Nonviolent communication works by avoiding language that psychologically creates defensiveness and instead promotes language that nurtures open mindedness and mutual understanding. It forces a person to slow down and think about how they are speaking before possibly making an emotionally violent situation even more violent. In Rosenberg's book, *Nonviolent Communication: A Language of Compassion*, he explains how to use observations, feelings, needs, and requests to navigate unmet needs you or others around you have (*Rosenberg 2002, 6*).

Stating unmet needs you have

1) Observe: What is it specifically that you like or don't like that a person is doing?

2) State your feelings: How does the observed action make you feel? Does it make you feel happy, alive, afraid, bored, detached, angry, calm, etc.? Remember that a feeling is not a judgment; do not use slander or make accusations.

3) State your needs. As mentioned previously, common human needs include sustenance, safety, love, empathy, rest (recreation and play), community, creativity, autonomy (freedom), and meaning (purpose): What is your unmet need from this list? Why do you personally want this change? How does it benefit you? Does it create more

order, make work go faster, create a quieter space, make a higher quality product, etc.? Needs explain your feelings.

4) Make a request: Make it clear, polite, reasonable, and preferably a "do" instead of a "don't." Remember, you are making a request, not a demand. "Could you please rewrite this with more action language," or, "can you start doing the dishes after you finish eating?"

5) Example: "Alex, when you play your electric guitar past 10:00 PM (observation), I feel frustrated (feeling) because I need to wake up for work early (need). Could you keep your playing to before 10:00 PM (request)?

Stating unmet needs others have

In conflicts, it is important to understand why another person believes what they do. You can use nonviolent communication to figure out another person's needs and make them more likely to listen to your own:

1) Observe and listen: What is the person expressing they like or dislike? This may be different than what that person initially states it is, or what you believe it to be.

2) Clarifying question: Make sure the person knows you understand what they like or dislike and the reason why. You may not agree with them, but it is important that a person feels that you are listening and can empathize. You may have to ask several clarifying questions to get to the root of the matter.

3) Your turn: Once the other person feels adequately heard, you can state your own feelings and needs or ask to offer advice.

Using non-judgmental language

Phrasing sentences nonviolently requires using non-judgmental language. Many words commonly used to describe feelings are actually evaluations of the other person, or how their actions are interpreted. This includes words such as "attacked, cheated, manipulated, provoked, rejected," and "unwanted" (*Rosenberg 2002, 44*). Judgmental language can be replaced with pure emotional states such as angry or sad.

Part of using non-judgmental language also involves not jumping to conclusions and instead considering the many reasons for a person acting the way that they did, or trying to connect with a person by asking them about their needs as explained previously. When asking these questions, do not blame yourself by using "I" language. For instance, instead of saying, "When I yelled at you . . ." try using "When people yell at you . . ." This helps prevent a person from feeling re-triggered from your actions and instead focus on their broader reality.

Suggestions for using non-violent communication effectively

- Keep your sentences short and simple so it is easier for people to listen.

- Ask people to "do" instead of "not do."

- Think about what you're going to say before you say it, or even write it out beforehand.

- Never make an assumption about why a person does something. Only speak from observable facts and clarify the truth by asking questions.

- To practice NVC go back to conversations that haven't gone so well in the past and rewrite them using non-violent communication.

All components of the non-violent communication model (observation, feelings, needs, requests) are needed or the interaction can quickly become either violent or misunderstood. However, words may be rephrased to sound more natural. For instance the example with Alex and the electric guitar could be phrased, "Alex, I've been hearing you play your electric guitar late (observation), and while I appreciate that you are falling in love with music, I've been getting frustrated and cranky (feeling) because I wake up for work early (need). Could you keep your playing to before 10:00PM (request)?"

· · ·

Life Mapping

How do you use language compared to others in writing and verbal communication? How do you handle conflicts?

POWERING UP YOUR BODY MOTIONS

*T*he body is a vessel for expression and communication. Every aspect of our bodies and the things we put on it alters our appearance and movements, thus conveying non-verbal information and casting spells on any onlooker, including ourselves. These spells can boost self-esteem, help build friendships and attract potential lovers, mark your belonging to a particular wizard clan, increase your physical capabilities, prevent diseases and other health problems, and much more.

While learning motion magic, it is useful to watch how workshop presenters, professional orators, and people you respect conduct themselves in conversation. A mirror is also quite useful for practicing particular spells. Naturally this won't allow you to see the effects, but you can get an idea of whether or not you are using the correct motions and gestures to successfully cast the desired spell. If you want to see the end results of your motion spells, you'll need to either seek feedback from people or record a video of yourself speaking, either while hanging out with people, alone, or giving a workshop. Timing, delivery, the wizard clans you are moving around, and what other spells such as words you are casting, all dictate the meaning of your motion spells.

Boost Confidence and Self-Esteem

Mental suffering may be triggered by stressful events or their approach. When you have the time, prepare by boosting your confidence and self-esteem. As wizard Amy Cuddy says, "fake it till you make it!" For instance, look into a mirror and talk yourself up while posing powerfully, or play the part of a great orator. What will also help boost confidence and self-esteem, as well as help you play this role, is dressing in a way that makes you feel good about yourself. Pick clothing, a hairstyle, and makeup that is intentional and fits the situation. "Fake it till you make it" means that it's possible to use simple techniques like these until, over time, you aren't just faking confidence, you are more confident and you do have better self-esteem. Remember that nothing will happen unless you first try.

Exercise

As mentioned in MAGICAL ACTIVITIES, physical exercise has numerous benefits to the practitioner including decreasing depression and anxiety, lessening the risk of disease, and improving overall health. Exercise can also be social such as playing a team sport. If you're a somewhat frail wizard or want to start off with something a little less taxing on the body, consider lighter forms of exercise like yoga, tai chi, or swimming. You can also combine physical activity with everyday tasks such as bicycling to work, squatting while brushing your teeth, using a yoga ball instead of an office chair or couch, or using a floor pedaling machine to move your legs while watching television.

Learn a Creative Movement

Many forms of creativity require movement, sometimes in the form of hand-eye coordination, and other times in balance, strength, and fine motor control. These all take time to develop, but can lead to beautiful creations through forms of drawing, painting, playing an instrument, dancing, spinning fire, and much more. You can read more about creative forms and making art under MAGICAL ACTIVITIES in ART AND CRAFT.

Fashion

Fashion is an art form: the clothing, makeup, hair, jewelry, tattoos, and other items you put on your body all influence the appearance of your movements and thus your spells as well. Do you want to look serious, colorful, formal, mysterious, sexy, or artsy? Ideally dress in a way that makes you feel good about yourself, but you can also wear clothing that reflects who you want to be seen as or what conforms to the wizard clan you want to impress. All of these factors lend to weaving a spell around onlookers, and even onto yourself.

Facial Gestures

Facial gestures alone can communicate questions, feelings, and more depending on the raise of an eyebrow, amount of teeth shown in a smile, or furrow of the forehead. Developing an emotionally neutral face or knowing how to act out certain facial gestures in appropriate situations can greatly help you win people over or strike fear into their souls.

Eye contact itself is an intimate connection that can show affection or aggression.

Our bodies actually associate smiling with expressing positive feelings and happiness (*Lienhard*). Even if you aren't feeling happy, try giving a genuine smile and you might at least have a small break from negative emotions. Also try putting yourself in a social situation where other people are around because smiling is actually a social cue used to express approval (*Ruiz-Belda 2003*). Laughing has a similar association.

General Body Motions

While not as essential as facial gestures are in communicating with people, other body motions are useful for accentuating statements. Raising your arms above your head might convey power or tiredness. Flipping your hands over can mean you are revealing something in conversation. Skipping up and down or dancing to a beat speaks to playfulness and high energy. Nervously twitching and shaking conveys nervousness or instability. These and many other body motions can all lend to either creating a dramatic and beautiful effect, or looking really awkward and strange. Again, observe, practice, and record yourself.

Positive Touch

If you can successfully use the right spells, it might lead you to finding yourself in some kind of intimate situation. Positive touch is any touch, sexual or non-sexual, that all parties enjoy. Part of the magic at work here is the vulnerability of touch—initiating or receiving it requires a great amount of trust. When that trust is met with respect it creates joy, comfort, and a deepened sense of connection.

Beyond the various partner dancing venues you can attend, some areas also have cuddle parties and free hugging sessions that can help connect you with people also seeking positive platonic touch. Many of the tips found in ROMANTIC RELATIONSHIPS under GROUP SPELLS AND MAGICAL ALLIES can be used for initiating platonic or sexual touch with others. Beyond those, each wizard clan has their own protocol for positive touch, which can also be unique between different individuals as well. Some people give touch freely, some like receiving touch in a specific way, and some don't like touch at all. In general you should keep in mind:

- Most people want to be asked before being touched, especially if they don't know you. This is known as consent. While this can require more vulnerability on your part, especially in rationally vocalizing an emotional desire, it ensures that both parties are going to enjoy the intimacy and increases the chance of the intimacy happening again or deepening into something more.

- If a person does want touch, they generally want touch in a particular way, so you may need to be reserved with your actions or at least ask follow up questions. For instance with hugging, some people want a long, tight, chest to chest hug, and other people want a short, light hug with plenty of space in between the two of you.

- If human intimacy is especially difficult for you to find, there are professional snugglers and sex workers who will touch you for a price.

- Most relationships and intimate content you see in media, especially in movies, is fictitious in nature and typically represents unhealthy, unrealistic, and non-consensual relationships. They are not good guides for how to get positive touch or into a relationship. Instead, read informational books or listen to personal accounts of romantic endeavors.

- Wizard clan protocols for intimacy are not always healthy, as they can make the requirements for receiving intimacy so high that only people with excruciatingly specific bodies, appearances, or personalities are able to receive it. However, these protocols do exist, especially for kissing, cuddling, and sex, and either need to be followed or transformed into something different (see ACTIVISM AND ALCHEMIZING THE MAGIC OF OTHER WIZARDS under MAGIC ALCHEMY). Things are changing however, especially because of several activist movements.

Familiars, or pets, such as cats and dogs can also act as good cuddle-partners, and will likely cause you much less drama than a human companion would. Research has found that contact with an animal improves comfort, increases feelings of safety, decreases depression and anxiety, lowers blood pressure and stress, and even helps create trust between patients and medical professionals (*Jackson 2013, 509-514*). Furthermore, familiars help teach you about compassionate behavior, an essential skill for developing friendships and relationships. If you can't have your own cat, dog, horse, or the like, consider going to a pet spa or animal shelter to spend some time with those cute critters. There are also pet therapy programs with horses, or doctors can even prescribe you a cat for dealing with anxiety.

•   •   •

Life Mapping

In what ways do you move your body? How do you receive positive touch in your life or what are some methods that you can add in more?

POWERING UP YOUR ENERGY

*M*agic ability is heavily influenced by various energies inherent in all wizards. Your energies dictate how many spells you can cast, but may also control the size of those spells. These factors make your energies crucial to your total magic potential (see GROWING YOUR MAGIC POTENTIAL under CONTROLLING YOUR MAGIC). Your primary energies can be broken up into emotional, mental, physical, and spiritual forms.

- Emotional energy: includes how you express feelings, the state of your mental health, and your typical mood.

- Mental energy: allows you to control your thoughts, process information, focus, and be creative.

- Physical energy: includes your capacity to perform physical tasks, how awake or sleepy you are, and how much physical movement you make.

- Spiritual energy: manifests through how you use all forms of magic, your morals and ethics, belief in something that exists beyond objective truth, openness to possibility, a deep connection with everyday objects and experiences, as well as being aware of spiritual energy.

Using a spell depletes the energy or energies it is associated with, making the consecutive casting of spells progressively more difficult. Energies can also be linked together, and you may have trouble casting all types of spells if even just one of your energies has run out. It is therefore important to know how to restore your energies, or at the very least how much you'll need to accomplish your essential tasks for a day. Your energy capacity can be improved with proper training, but can also weaken with neglect. In the most direct example, physical energy increases if you exercise but diminishes if you stop. In exercising an energy, you use up some of it temporarily but gain an increased amount after you've rested.

Depending on the amount you've exercised an energy and several other factors like your biology and upbringing, you may have a high, medium, or low capacity for a particular energy type. Having a high amount of one of these energies does not necessarily mean you are skilled with the associated type of magic though, just that you have a greater capacity to use more of it. There are also many things which may block your ability to fully use your stored energy, such as forms of the darkness like depression and trauma.

While it becomes harder to cast certain spells once you've used up an energy type, you may surprise yourself with hidden stores of energy you never knew existed if you push yourself. This frequently happens if you care deeply about something or someone, such as with winning a race or working through a difficult conversation. The same may be true if you're feeling too exhausted to go to an event like a social gathering, the new environment might give you a burst of energy instead of tiring you out.

Energies are often not apparent to others except through indirect observation over an extended period of time. For instance, a person may initially appear physically energetic but simply be energetic in that moment and actually have fairly low physical energy. Likewise, simply because a person meditates or attends church does not immediately make that person have strong spiritual energy. People may be high energy in some areas and low energy in others.

Your energy interacts with other energies. Some energies may be exciting like a new face at work or being sexually attracted to someone, but others may be overwhelming like loud music when you're sleepy. Appropriately interacting with the energy will help make the energetic exchange tolerable or enjoyable for yourself. You can:

- Flow with the energy—a form of acceptance such as talking with or stepping closer to it.

- Change the energy—transform the energy in oneself with things like joking, leaving, or talking.

- Ignore the energy—avoid the energy present. You can do this by playing music, a game, or finding another conversation.

Each instance must be individually considered to reach your ideal level of comfort. Approaching an energy encroaching on your space is best done lovingly with questions or nonviolent communication. You do not want to make the energy defensive, or it may become a more intense energy. You can also ask yourself if the source of energy is the problem or if your predisposed beliefs, mental blocks, and traumas are at issue. Different people may find nourishment using different techniques, or they may be more skilled at one over another.

Restoring Energy and Sleep

Each energy type has a multitude of ways of being restored that is unique to the individual. I can provide some general restorative methods, but you'll have to explore what works for you personally. Introverted and highly sensitive wizards especially will have to experiment with what works and what doesn't when confronted with overwhelm and exhaustion (see INTROVERTS AND EXTROVERTS under TYPES OF WIZARDS). Some options include:

- Eating an energizing and nutritious meal.

- Taking a break or going on vacation.

- Looking at nature.

- Turning off your phone and keeping your eyes off screens.

- Being alone or quiet.

- Socializing with people who you enjoy.

- Taking a nap.

- Meditating.

- Doing something you find relaxing like drinking tea or watching a show.

- Being somewhere peaceful.

- Immersing yourself in beauty.

Of course, the most important method by which energy is restored is a proper amount of sleep. During sleep the body repairs itself, long-term memories are stored, and the mind is allowed to take a break from difficult thoughts and struggles. There is no exact amount of sleep any individual needs, although too much or too little sleep is associated with several health problems (*National Sleep Foundation*). A healthy amount of sleep for adults is 7 to 9 hours per day, for teenagers 8.5 to 9.25 hours per day, and 5 to 10 year-olds 10 to 11 hours per day. Keep in mind that tiredness can act as a trigger for negative feelings from not sleeping enough, sleeping too much, eating certain foods, or performing physically and mentally strenuous activities. Listen to your body and allow it the amount of rest it really needs.

To sleep better:

- Take a natural sleep aid such as chamomile, melatonin, or valerian.

- Avoid viewing electronic media within a few hours before sleep. The screen interacts with your brain in such a way that it makes your sleep less restful and makes it more difficult to fall asleep (*Trapani 2007*). You can download a screen filter or wear glasses that block blue light to help prevent being wakeful from screens.

- Exercising in the morning or midday helps with falling asleep later, but don't exercise at night; it makes falling asleep harder (*Trapani 2007*). That said, if you are having trouble sleeping, you can do a light physical activity to try to burn off some of the energy.

- Foods such as warm milk, bananas, potatoes, oatmeal, and whole-wheat bread help induce sleep (*Trapani 2007*).

- Make sleeping a routine with brushing your teeth, flossing, changing into pajamas, and maybe a small activity as part of it. Go to bed and wake up at the same time each day, and only use your bed for sleeping and sex, not working in. By using a routine like this, your body will know it is time to sleep (*Smith, Melinda et al. 2011*).

- Only nap earlier in your day and keep naps to below 30 minutes (*Smith, Melinda et al. 2011*).

- Only expose yourself to dim light when you're ready for bed to allow the level of melatonin, the natural sleep hormone, to increase and tell the body it is time to sleep (*Smith, Melinda et al. 2011*). Note that the light from a full moon diminishes your quality of sleep and makes it harder to fall asleep as well (*Cajochen 2013*). It can be useful to wear a sleep mask to block light and help sleep.

- Make your bedroom a comfortable space by eliminating noises, keeping it dark, and maintaining a temperature of 65 degrees Fahrenheit or below *(Smith, Melinda et al. 2011)*.

- Eat enough that you don't get hungry before sleeping, but don't eat big meals, drink large amounts of liquids, or consume alcohol late at night. Smoking at all or drinking caffeine a few hours past when you wake up both make it harder to sleep and diminish your quality of sleep *(Smith, Melinda et al. 2011)*.

- Stress can prevent you from sleeping *(Smith, Melinda et al. 2011)*. Sometimes when I can't sleep or am obsessing over a thought, going into a state of meditation and only focusing on deep breathing helps me fall asleep.

- If you wake up in the middle of the night, worrying about being able to fall back asleep will only keep you awake *(Smith, Melinda et al. 2011)*. Try to relax thoughtlessly or do a calm activity such as reading for a little while.

- Avoid putting disturbing or stressful things in your mental scope such as horror movies. At least for myself, these stimuli increase the chance that I have nightmares and diminish my quality of sleep. Not only that, but also once experienced, they stay with you for the rest of your life. Be considerate of what you want your memories to be composed of.

- Listen to soothing recorded background sounds like rain, wind, and ocean waves to help mask or block noises that keep you awake. You can find noise generating applications online and for smartphones. You can also turn on a fan or wear earplugs.

- Homeschool your children or petition schools to start later in the morning. This allows you to start brain activities at a more reasonable hour and help both you and your children get more sleep!

- Get a job that allows you to sleep in later, or work for yourself.

To wake up and stay energized:

- Eat foods that contain protein and fat instead of just carbohydrates and sugar. Eating fruit or carbohydrates like bread alone will increase your energy short term and then create a sugar crash, causing tiredness (Newitz 2007).

- If you use an alarm clock, set it away from your bed so you have to get up to turn it off.

- Do a light exercise and stretch for 5 to 10 minutes within an hour of waking up. This pairs nicely with mindfulness practices. In the short term doing the exercises will wake your body up, in the longer term your body will associate waking up with being prepared for activity.

- Get a consistent amount of sleep each night and don't oversleep.

- Expose yourself to lots of light, preferably direct sunlight, in the morning to lower levels of the natural sleep hormone, melatonin (Smith, Melinda et al. 2011).

- Try to get outside and moving within an hour of waking up.

- Drink tea or coffee (note that some people crash several hours after drinking a caffeinated beverage).

- Shower in the morning instead of at night.

- Eat a more nutritious diet.

- Keep windows open or get outside throughout the day. The buildup of CO_2 in a room with no airflow can cause drowsiness (*Wisconsin Department of Health Services 2013*).

In order to find a healthy energy balance, some people need to release or calm their energy first. This is often the case when a wizard feels overwhelmed, stressed, anxious, or uncomfortable. While releasing energy is fairly straightforward, it may be difficult to find a place that feels comfortable to do so. Consider going on a run, yelling into a pillow, crying, making art, or listening to loud music. Various techniques can also be used to calm your energy levels, such as meditation, being in nature, walking barefoot on the earth, taking a bath, or smelling pleasant aromas.

Now how do you power up your physical, mental, emotional, and spiritual energies? Physical energy is covered in POWERING UP YOUR MOTIONS. Mental energy is covered extensively in several sections including POWERING UP YOUR MIND AND THOUGHTS, COPING WITH THE DARKNESS, and THE SUBCONSCIOUS.

Emotional Energy

Mastery of your emotional energy will greatly enhance your spells with the ability to enter into your chosen emotional state at will or transform unwanted emotional energy. The appropriate use of emotions can help you express talking points better, make a person laugh, enjoy life, release unwanted negative energy, protect yourself from harm, and fall in love. This energy is expressed through your body motions and tone of voice, so read up in POWERING UP YOUR BODY MOTIONS and POWERING UP YOUR WORDS. Here we will further explore what influences your emotional energy as well as several more techniques to gain greater control over this energy type.

Reconnecting With Your Emotional Self

Many people have learned to suppress their emotions due to cultural norms, trauma, or not receiving a supportive upbringing during childhood. While expressing emotions is a vulnerable act, experiencing the full range of emotions holds one key to living a fulfilling life. Suppressing your emotions may also lead them to becoming trapped in your body in the form of trauma and be immensely uncomfortable. Your emotions may be suppressed if you have trouble crying when feeling sad, experiencing beauty, committing to relationships, or feeling love for others. To open your emotional self you can:

- Surround yourself with emotionally open people. Accomplish this through dating someone or joining a community that expresses their emotions openly.

- Form a deep sense of trust with a person and be more vulnerable. While this may be a slow process, you can also expedite it through various activities or bonding experiences.

- Confront what you fear or what made you cut off your emotional side. This might be a parental figure, a childhood bully, or someone you dated. You don't necessarily have to directly confront these sources, just the energy and self-limiting beliefs that they produced within yourself.

Emotional Mastery

Most of this book relates directly or indirectly to the mastery of your emotions. You can brush up on some of these techniques by reading CONTROLLING YOUR MAGIC, MAGICAL ACTIVITIES, COPING WITH THE DARKNESS, and POWERING UP YOUR MIND AND THOUGHTS. Here are a few more techniques as well:

Deal with the negative emotions you have about yourself and others as soon as possible

Suffering is an important aspect of life. Growth and knowledge is found in these difficulties, and so it is generally good to work through it. In fact, avoiding dealing with negative emotions directed toward yourself or another person can quickly pull the whole mind into a state of depressed feelings or depression. Often the longer you wait to deal with these feelings, the harder the situation becomes to remedy and the worse the suffering becomes (granted, some time is necessary to process thoughts and react constructively to a situation).

What do I mean by avoiding dealing with negative emotions? It is the lack of making a decision. Communicating with a friend, accepting certain qualities of a person, quitting a job, practicing mindfulness, or ending a relationship would all be potentially beneficial decisions. Complaining, venting, doing nothing, or obsessing over the negative qualities of a situation would constitute avoidance. Be proactive about your mental health.

As for altering negative feelings toward another person, you can use previously explored techniques, either communicating to the person you're upset with using nonviolent communication, or forgiving that person. Some personalities don't get along, but plenty more do. Why dwell on the negative when there are so many positive things to be experienced? Whenever your mind starts making a judgment or saying something hateful, say something nice, and focus on that instead. Remind yourself that thinking hateful thoughts or making judgments is not helping anyone or teaching anyone a better method of being, and generally just hurts you. Since you cannot change what happened, you may as well be content or happy with the idea that the universe meant it to happen for your personal story. Whether out of difficulty or happiness, regret gets you nowhere. Of course, you can learn from regret and act differently in the future, but right now, why dwell on the past?

For complaints and negative thinking that continuously arise in yourself, consider setting aside time to fully allow those feelings and thoughts to be vented. For instance, release all that pent up energy for 15 minutes, and then visualize putting it into a box. If the complaints try to come out again, remind those thoughts that you already gave them enough of your time today. Repeat this process once per day as needed. Alternatively you can also visualize a wall that keeps you safe from your sources of stress.

Accept what you fear

Many feelings are absolutely rational, but others create unnecessary strife and misdirect where action is needed to feel better. Underlying feelings such as hatred, dislike, and jealousy are sometimes fear. By identifying this root emotion you take responsibility for external or internal conflict and can challenge yourself to grow. There might be a fear of not being as good as someone else, being wrong, of a recurrence of a past event, being harmed, being emotionally hurt, or being embarrassed. Which of these fears are rational and which are irrational? Which can you transform? Which can you seek reassurance about?

Accepting the outcomes of certain fears can also allow you to move on and sprout happiness where once there was negativity. Many hobbies, habits, and thinking patterns result from the fear of what would happen if we did not do one thing or another. However, this creates a negative mindset when doing these things. Activities often pursued out of fear and negativity include exercise, social tendencies, dressing up, diets, activism, and careers.

If your actions are based on fear, work on accepting the worst possible outcome of not doing that thing. Instead of holding onto the fear, allow it to fully happen in your imagination. Generally this outcome really isn't that bad, and at the very worst is only one of thousands of possibilities that could happen. Holding onto one possibility that makes you feel bad is simply not productive. It might be helpful to even stop doing the fear-based activity altogether for a set period of time. Transform negative tendencies into positive ones by pursuing those activities out of enjoyment, happiness, love, or fulfillment. If you cannot alter these feelings, pursue different activities.

Love more

Love is a special symbiosis of trust, joy, and vulnerability. There are many types of love spells such as friendship, self-love, the love of a place or object, love of a nation or clan, and various kinds of romantic and sexual love. Love is the most powerful of positive magic spells, and its influence can quickly uplift the energies of the caster, target, and anyone in the immediate vicinity. Love's power creates happiness, fulfillment, sense of purpose, and is the strongest force available to fight against the darkness. Love is also contagious—the more that you fill yourself with the vibrant energy of love, the more those around you will love.

You can invite more love into your life by:

- Expressing gratitude to others and selflessly giving people thoughtful gifts.

- Spending meaningful social time with others.

- Supporting others emotionally.

- Dressing up in quirky, artistic, and fashionable ways.

- Smiling and laughing more.

- Focusing on building stronger connections with your family, friends, and romantic partners.

- Limiting or removing as many sources of the darkness as you can in your life including judgments, hatred, depression, and self-destructive tendencies (see COPING WITH THE DARKNESS).

- Being passionate about a particular interest or really good at a hobby that you can invite others to participate in.

- Surrounding yourself with people who are thriving and love openly.

- Becoming a central figure in your community or reaching your highest form (see A WIZARD'S HIGHEST FORM and GROUP SPELLS AND MAGICAL ALLIES).

- Attending social functions or hosting some yourself.

- Asking yourself in every social interaction, "how can I make this person's life better and this connection more amazing?"

- Knowing that every day is an opportunity to improve and grow your capacity to love.

As beneficial as learning love magic is to a person's well-being, love spells can be quite difficult to cast and unwieldy to maintain depending on the sort of love you attempt to weave. A failed love spell can create a lot of hardship or even overwhelm a person with the darkness. Love can also have unhealthy aspects, such as feeling overly possessive, expecting something in return for expressing your love, craving love which you do not or no longer have, or codependent love in which people neglect other healthy relationships for romantic love. Many wizards learn through experience how to avoid these difficult and emotionally draining forms of love, but learning from wizards who specialize in romantic relationships like certain therapists or authors may help you avoid these mishaps. You can read about the specifics of how to cast healthy love spells in GROUP SPELLS AND MAGICAL ALLIES.

Vulnerability and the health of stress, sadness, and anger

As you explore coping with forms of mental suffering, you may attempt to avoid situations that create "negative" feelings. Know however that these are all parts of the human experience, and avoiding them is to avoid learning, growing, and even experiencing many positive aspects of life. When we try to avoid an emotion, we numb all of our emotions. Sometimes it is the negative or difficult experiences that make us find our happiness. Sometimes things just need to get really bad before you find the motivation to make changes in your life, or before you finally understand advice you heard years ago.

Uncomfortable situations provide a lot of motivation for creating constructive changes in our lives. Seeing them as opportunities, rather than tragedies to be kept secret from ourselves, is essential to rediscovering a content and happy place. Welcome stress in as a challenge to grow from and overcome. Of course, some suffering is just too much to address, and you may need to revisit it later once you have taken care of the immediate difficulties associated with that pain.

Spiritual Energy

Unlike your other forms of energy, spiritual energy is difficult to describe because it does not have a particular physical form and is composed of every aspect of a person's unique existence. It is most prominently a way of being. Not everyone taps into this source of energy, but doing so grants a greater ability to perform strenuous and emotionally exhausting tasks while maintaining commitments and being able to derive profound insights and fulfillment from everyday events.

Spiritual energy does not require that you believe in things that transcend the knowledge found in scientific inquiry, but does require believing in something more than yourself. This could be the metaphors that stories tell, nature, possibility, the interconnected energies of people and the universe, god(s), or various other powers. These beliefs contain great magic and are the source of spiritual energy.

The sum of all your spiritual energy makes up your soul. All humans are born with a soul, but it may have difficulty expressing itself due to:

- Media consumption
- Unrequited feelings
- Fears
- Too many to-dos
- Addictions
- Valuing logic over emotions
- Notions of absolute truth in right, wrong, good, and evil

Developing spiritual energy is a means of exposing and befriending the soul. When nothing impedes the soul's way, the soul will integrate with your personality and grant you bountiful beauty, serendipitous surprises and cosmic gifts. You can build your spiritual energy through:

- Play

- Expressing emotions

- Meditation

- Being present and aware of your inner and outer environment

- Connecting to basic human needs

- Being in nature

- Growing food

- Loving people

- Making art

- Knowing the pinnacles of darkness and depths of light

- Being in silence

Spiritual energy can also be derived from a deep belief and commitment to a source of magic. There are many forms that this can take on, but some common ones are listed below.

Environmental stewardship

Accessing spiritual energy from nature takes more than just doing good deeds for the environment, it takes seeing yourself as part of nature and the vast organism that the Earth makes up. Examples of this can be found in certain diet forms whether vegan, vegetarian, pescatarian, omnivore, etc. So long as the consumer is making decisions about how they eat based on sustainable principles, they have built an environmental connection. Other examples of working with natural connections include: visiting nature, cleaning up your city, growing your own food, using biodegradable products, buying used products, and limiting the amount of fossil fuels you use.

Spiritual or religious groups

There are hundreds of spiritual and religious groups to join that tap into spiritual energy, though of course, some niche groups may be more difficult to find in smaller cities. Pick one or even a few that resonate with you. However, be careful about appropriating what another culture finds sacred without the proper research and respect. This often takes the form of studying with a particular group of wizards belonging to that spiritual culture. Appropriated culture tends to have much weaker spiritual energy as it disregards the full meaning and energies contained within an act or object.

Community

Spiritual energy may be created through a community working closely together toward a common goal. It helps living among people that you enjoy, or people that you resonate with energetically. Some of this energy can also be manifested by knowing the producers of your goods through buying locally made products. See COMMUNITIES under GROUP SPELLS AND MAGICAL ALLIES.

Befriending yourself

Being your own best friend will greatly help you develop spiritually. This requires a commitment to working on all aspects of yourself while loving and accepting who you are now, including your shadow. Your shadow includes all those hidden parts of yourself that you find less than desirable like your judgments, self-doubts, regrets, hypocritical actions, mistakes, vices, shortcomings, and the other things that may lead to a negative or self-destructive mindset. Even though these may be aspects of yourself you seek to work on, they are still part of your humanity. Read more about your Shadow in YOUR SHADOW AND LIGHT FORMS under THE SUBCONSCIOUS.

You can also visualize the energy within specific parts of your body to determine what needs healing or improvement. There are many tools you can do this with but people most often use chakras (originating from India) or meridian systems (originating from China). Western teachings on these systems are considerably different than other parts of the world, but you can still learn the basics from yoga, acupuncture, and several forms of meditation. More advanced education will require books, articles, formal education, or travel abroad. You can also simply focus on an area of your body and inquire into how it feels from your toes up through your head. If you're not feeling well in your body, consider applying some of the exercises explored in POWERING UP YOUR BODY MOTIONS or consuming different magic potions, explored in MAGIC POTIONS.

Exploring the subconscious

Your subconscious and spiritual energy is deeply connected. Making art, meditating, and paying closer attention to your dreams can help nurture a pathway to the soul. Read more in THE SUBCONSCIOUS.

Tune in with nature's rhythms

Nature follows many cycles throughout the year. You can see these with changes in light, weather, astral movements, hormones, color, and the cycle of life and death. Transcribing these rhythms into your life, as well as discovering what your own natural rhythms are will help open the spiritual energies found in nature into your soul. You can incorporate these cycles into your life with things such as moon journals or almanacs, or take on activities such as gardening and hiking.

Now that you understand how to power up some of your magic, let's explore the destructive spells and forms of the darkness that might be impeding your way to acquiring your highest form of being.

•   •   •

Life Mapping

How strong are your mental, physical, spiritual, and emotional energies? How can you power up these energies?

DESTRUCTIVE SPELLS THAT WIZARDS ARE COMMONLY UNDER

Wizards are actively controlled by many spells. Some of these are quite beneficial and healthy, such as having a habit of exercising or having a tendency to see the good in people. Other spells are quite destructive to a wizard clan or individual such as addictions, jealousy, and certain thinking patterns. If you carry any of these destructive spells, consider whether or not they are helping you or your clan's well-being. If they aren't, it might be time to reconsider the idea and foster more positive spells. Learn how to do this in HABITS AND AUTOCASTING MAGIC SPELLS under CONTROLLING YOUR MAGIC and MAGIC ALCHEMY. It is especially important to confront destructive spells as the existence of one will often breed more and consume a person or group of people with suffering.

Blocking Destructive Spells

A destructive spell cast by a wizard or group of wizards can be blocked or countered with a variety of techniques. Destructive spells range in type—some consume you with negative thoughts and feelings, some manipulate your actions and ideas to support a particular wizard clan, and some make you form addictions to dangerous substances. In general these spells take over your reality, and can either come externally from other sources or internally from your own thoughts and behaviors.

Destructive spells are easiest to fall into when we are lacking or insecure about something. In order to try to protect ourselves or fill in what is missing, we become reactionary and take on anything that seems immediately beneficial to our well-being. It's quite easy for destructive spells to be masked underneath seemingly positive magic as well—for instance a group of friends may peer pressure you into forming an unhealthy addiction or to do something mean to another person. This is why becoming aware of destructive spells is essential.

Your awareness of destructive spells will largely come from your own personal experiences, but listening to knowledgeable wizards may also clue you into things to avoid. Seeing what else is possible is most easily accomplished by traveling to foreign countries, attending art and music festivals, or visiting free-thinking spaces such as intentional communities, liberal arts and alternative universities, and personal growth workshops.

Until you get hurt by certain destructive spells though, the positive mask that exists over them may be too tempting to resist. Of course, a spell may be beneficial to one wizard but destructive to another, so it is up to you to decide. You should be aware however that many wizard clans are embedded with destructive spells which greatly increase individual experiences of the darkness, even if no one is scrutinizing that aspect of your culture.

Once you are aware of a destructive spell being cast on you, you can then work on preventing it from consuming your reality. This might involve avoiding unwanted activities, using mindfulness meditation, making art, playing a game or watching a show, reminding yourself of what is important in your life, going on a walk, or just generally ignoring the destructive spell.

These methods can take a lot of emotional energy and self-control, so sometimes the easier approach is to lower the occurrence of destructive spells being flung your way altogether. This can be done by finding a healthy environment to surround yourself with that includes supportive friends and community, natural spaces, animal companions, art, good communication, and people who seek personal growth and take care of their bodies. You can also build environments like this where you currently live, it might just be difficult depending on the dominant culture. Many areas do have support groups where you can temporarily find relief from destructive spells too.

Destructive spells can also be countered. You have to be careful with using a destructive spell against another destructive spell though. Often using one of these spells will cause the user to suffer as well—and if the target is adept at blocking or re-countering destructive spells, your attempts will have been meaningless and have put you into an even worse mood. That said, it can be beneficial, especially in self-defense or when used with a group of people calling out a behavior as bad. A more likely way to feel good is by using constructive magic to counter the spell. For instance, smiling at a person who curses you, giving them a compliment, showing empathy, having a kind and compassionate conversation, or asking questions about that person's beliefs. These will often leave you feeling better, help transform the destructive spell caster, and potentially lead to a positive connection.

Curses

Curses are negative statements made about other people, either when talking about the person or speaking directly to them. These are often cast with an intent of revenge, increasing one's social status, or belittling a person for a perceived mistake. Curses are typically ineffective at creating real change in a person other than potentially making them feel terrible and strongly disliking the spell caster. Another drawback is that curses tend to consume the caster with negative energy.

If someone attempts to curse you, it tends not to do much to try and curse them back. Instead you can deflect curses in a number of ways:

- Say to yourself, "I don't believe that about myself."

- Use a safe word or meditate away from negative thoughts caused by the curse.

- Have empathy and say to yourself, "that person must be going through a really hard time."

- Say to yourself "I return this curse to its sender." Anytime the memory of the curse arises, repeat this line.

- Do the opposite of what the person expects—smile at them, laugh, or say thank you.

If you find yourself cursing others frequently and want to stop:

- Remove yourself from the source of stress.

- Be proactive about fixing your problems by using things like nonviolent communication to talk with a person.

- Realize your part in why you want to curse this person— maybe you have a personal sensitivity or grew up in a culture different from this person. Maybe you are being defensive and are refusing to acknowledge your fault in the matter.

- Rewire your brain to be more positive.

- Realize the amount of time and energy you are wasting by being negative.

- Have empathy and consider why this person behaves the way they do.

- If you catch yourself cursing someone, breathe deeply and practice mindfulness to bring yourself back to the present moment. You can even just start naming off objects in your surroundings to ground yourself back in reality.

- Seek out a therapist to help guide you through exercises to release some of your pent up energy around a person.

- Instead of silently flinging curses while avoiding a person, have a normal conversation with them instead, or just ask them a simple question. Sometimes this can help remind you that they are not always an awful person.

- Use visualization or a safe word that draws you back into pleasant thoughts. This might include things like the name and image of a loved one or a happy memory.

- Learn how to forgive a person in FORGIVENESS under POWERING UP YOUR MIND AND THOUGHTS.

Stereotypes

Stereotypes have been used over time to push violent and oppressive agendas against marginalized religions, people of color, women, and many other groups. It is important to ask yourself when you hear a generalization about a group of people whether or not it might in fact be a stereotype and only represent a portion of a population. Many stereotypes are actually distorted versions of the truth and represent almost no portion of a population at all.

Discrimination

Discrimination is the act of treating a group of people negatively or excluding them because you perceive something about them as unlikable. This separation is unfortunately quite easy for the brain to do with hardly any reason. The brain loves homogeneous environments because they create a sense of familiar safety, like in tribal communities. However, because humans rarely live in stable environments these days, it forces the brain to either accept and respect the unfamiliar energies or feel stressed out by their existence. This creates an "us" versus "them" mentality.

Discrimination often utilizes inaccurate stereotypes of a group of people in order to make it easier to judge them as a whole and further put your distance between your clans. Wizards commonly discriminate against other people because of race, skin color, language, age, biological sex, sexual orientation, gender, appearance, religious beliefs, and ability to perform tasks.

Many forms of discrimination arise from wizard clans with contradicting ideologies trying to coexist in the same space. Due to the strong disagreements some of these cultures have, or the vastly different ways in which they communicate, it can be difficult for them to get along with others. Furthermore, when multiple cultures inhabit the same area, it limits how any culture can be expressed. Instead, cultures have to exist in microcosms where enough support exists, and people are often limited in the extent to which they can fully celebrate who they identify as in those spaces.

Discrimination can also persist with inaccurate beliefs being passed down from generation to generation, or instilled cultural beliefs. These can include things such as societal rules and gender norms. Although it can be difficult and time consuming, there are several ways to dispel discrimination:

- Work towards creating laws to protect the people being discriminated against.

- Volunteer at or research how to create social welfare programs for people going through difficult times as well as mothers who must take time off of work to raise a newborn child.

- Inform people about how their stereotypes are inaccurate.

- Introduce more diversity into your area and have children who grow up with cultural diversity being a part of everyday life.

- Petition lawmakers and internet providers to prevent censorship on the internet. An uncensored internet greatly helps diversity spread by exposing people to the global diversity of ideas and cultures. Unfortunately nearly all search engines and social media platforms use algorithms that make a user's biased opinions appear first.

- Give people spaces to celebrate their unique cultures within. If acceptable, invite people not belonging to that culture in to participate.

- Prevent false information from spreading that promotes discrimination. Be sure to check your sources before sharing news articles online.

- Be friendly to people who have a discriminatory attitude toward you, disprove their assumptions and contradict how they think you'll act.

- Create a common sense of unity surrounding a shared need such as reversing climate change or ending discrimination.

Read more in ACTIVISM AND ALCHEMIZING THE MAGIC OF OTHER WIZARDS under MAGIC ALCHEMY.

Hierarchies

Hierarchies can be quite beneficial in effective organizing and ensuring tasks are completed. However, by placing some people as more important than others, hierarchies often ignore or degrade the essential roles that many people play within a group. Remember that everyone has a unique intelligence and is capable of a lot if empowered to do so. For that reason, members and employees will be much happier if they have some say in the decision making process and are given fair treatment and wages.

Controlling more power than others can also corrupt a person's ability to empathize and show compassion. Leaders may even be forced to act in ways which prioritizes efficiency first and lead to treating followers disrespectfully. Employee and worker-owned collectives help resolve some of these problems.

Economic and Monetary Systems

Most societies use a form of economic or monetary system in order to make transactions between people easier. Many wizards take for granted that these systems are flexible and not actually essential to their livelihood. Instead of sharing resources, growing food, or having the basic skills to create an article of clothing or tool, wizards get caught up making major life decisions in order to collect more money while often going into debt. Simultaneously, wizards are convinced of doing really strange things in the name of money that do not at all uplift or fulfill them. This often results in a wizard's personal well-being and highest form being neglected.

Competition

While competing against others can be fun, create motivation to try harder, and reward the brain with positive chemicals for winning, it also necessitates that there be losers. This can create a great amount of stress in striving to win, create negative feelings toward the opposition, and with too many losses, may turn a person away from an activity they otherwise enjoy. Fortunately alternatives exist that involve more cooperation. By working together, you increase your chances of succeeding, and even if you don't, losing together feels much less stressful. Some ways to build winners out of everyone include:

- Styles of voting that use consensus models in which everyone must agree before pushing a decision forward.

- Socialism and sharing economies, where everyone is supporting one another directly or through social welfare programs.

- Cooperative board games.

- Collectively buying food together or income sharing.

- Cultures whose neighborhoods communally construct houses.

Ego

Your ego represents your self-esteem and confidence. Having an inflated ego might make you believe that you're better than someone else. The truth is that there is no better or worse, there are just people with different personalities who you are judging from your lifetime of experiences and wizard clan's ideologies. In order to dispel this type of thinking, read POWERING UP YOUR MIND AND THOUGHTS.

Materialism

Materialism is the act of buying or otherwise acquiring things that you do not need in order gain a temporary feeling of joy. Some wizards are tricked by nations and businesses into believing that material wealth equates to happiness and well-being. This is true to a certain extent for living a comfortable life, but these wizards may spend their lives working jobs that they dislike or find no fulfillment in just to be able to afford more material possessions. This often pairs with ignoring the bountiful beauty of life found in love, friendships, nature, spirituality, and the arts. A better spell for promoting well-being while meeting material needs is sharing.

Instead of purchasing more stuff, could you spend your money on positive or memorable experiences and activities? At least check in with yourself about what you actually need. Often if you wait a few days before deciding on a purchase, you may realize you don't actually want the thing you were originally so enamored with. Understand that sellers are heavily influencing your psychology to buy immediately, so try not to be tempted by their spells of manipulation.

Store-bought items contain much less magical energy within them as well. This is somewhat helped with buying items from local crafters, but best is if someone gifts you the item or you make it yourself. The ability to simply go into a store and purchase something has disconnected people from understanding how objects are made. Learning crafting skills can be a lot of fun, improve your connection with your home environment, be spiritually powerful, and give you some great activities to do with friends.

Ownership

Ownership is an idea that exists within systems of materialism. No one can truly own anything because no one fully has control over the material world. A healthier way of looking at ownership is as a set of spells you've used to form a friendship, however temporary and impermanent, with an object. That means it should be fine if others also form spells of friendship with that same object, but hopefully respect the boundaries you have in that connection.

Color

Colors influence mood largely based on which clan a wizard belongs to. Color is not inherently destructive, but is often used intentionally or unintentionally in destructive ways. For instance, businesses use color to influence buyer's decisions in things they might not otherwise want or need. Many people also live in houses, wear clothing, and visit public spaces with color schemes that diminish rather than uplift their moods. In western clans, red can induce anxiety and stress, green is calming, and purple empowering. You can learn more about color by attending color theory and painting classes, or by reading books like *Color—Messages & Meanings* by Leatrice Eiseman or *The Complete Color Harmony, Pantone Edition* by Tina Sutton.

Attractiveness

Each wizard clan has a unique and constantly changing concept of what attractiveness and beauty mean to them. Many wizards believe a potential romance or even friendship relies on these physical characteristics or personality traits in order to be desirable. This is often unhealthy and untrue—Wizards who allow a diversity of body types and personalities into their lives begin to expand what they find attractive. This openness may require cutting out media, reading fashion magazines that portray a variety of body types, or not consuming pornography.

Self-Limiting Beliefs

Almost all wizards carry self-limiting beliefs and stories about what they are capable of. These might include things like: "I am not smart," "I am not attractive enough to date that person," "People don't like me." "I will always be anxious," or, "I am too shy for public speaking." Reframing these thoughts into more open-ended statements will greatly help you open your capacity to grow and learn new skills. For instance, for the examples above, you might say "I have had some trouble enjoying and focusing on mathematics," "I feel shy about asking that person out," "I want to cultivate stronger friendships," "I am learning coping mechanisms to handle my anxiety better," and, "I know that public speaking is a skill that I can become better at with practice and dedication." Read more in ALCHEMIZING YOUR PERSONAL MAGIC under MAGIC ALCHEMY.

The Individual

The individual is a concept which entertains the idea that a person can be strong, content, and capable by their effort alone. This is an entirely fictional and unhealthy concept, but is praised in many wizarding nations as a sign of status and power. While many people can make it by "alone," their ability to do so is based on hundreds or even thousands of people that the individual does not interact with, as well as the natural world that they extract resources from. Humans are social creatures that rely on one another. To believe otherwise is to ignore the need for friendship, love, community and the natural environment.

The Nuclear Family

The nuclear family includes parents and one or more child, typically living together without anyone else. It is the default social structure of most families, and while a goal of many people, frequently leads to a number of problems. Often children only have the support of their parents, who may be absent for work, abusive, or mentally incapable of giving support. Parents may be unable to take time off from raising their children, and cannot take a vacation or go on a date due to the costs of childcare. Children do not have multiple people to form ideas from and are separated from interacting with a wide range of ages. Lastly, parents may lack close relationships with people other than their nuclear family and lose contact with friends.

Healthier alternatives do exist. Multiple families can live together and share parenting duties. Families can live in communities with a diverse age range. Extended family can live together or nearby. Parents can explore polyamory in which multiple partners take responsibility for care of the children. These alternative structures allow much more support for children and the parents.

School

Schools, while at least partly effective in teaching some basic skills to growing wizards, tend to do so inefficiently and in ways which are uncomfortable for students, teachers, and parents. Many schools are understaffed and overcrowded, students have to wake up much earlier than makes sense for their natural rhythms, punishment is shame-based and negative, limited types of intelligence are promoted thus not allowing young wizards to excel at their unique and natural talents, and foundational skills are ignored such as creativity, effective communication, critical thinking, and self-care.

There are many improvements that can be made. The school population could be closer to one adult per one student, or no more than one adult to ten students. Student's unique interests and intelligences could be promoted. The mornings could start with meditation, dance, and positive affirmations. Healthy food could be served, even straight from educational gardens.

A variety of alternative educational structures do exist or are emerging that incorporate these solutions. For self-motivated individuals, you hardly even need a structure anymore with the amazing amount of content found online and in libraries to educate yourself. If you want to learn a skill, do an internet search, look up videos, or ask on a forum. Someone knows and wants to help you succeed.

Addiction and Greed

Addictions temporarily make a wizard feel better before causing symptoms of withdrawal, such as anxiety and depression or being consumed by the darkness. Addictions may take the form of substances, sensations, or media. People become wrapped in a spell of addiction much more easily when they are stressed and looking for an easy way to manage the resulting emotions. See ADDICTIVE MAGIC POTIONS under MAGIC POTIONS, or HABITS AND AUTOCASTING MAGIC SPELLS under CONTROLLING YOUR MAGIC.

Greed is one type of addiction in which people accumulate more than they need and refuse to share it with others, or make a decision which only benefits themselves. It often makes people feel powerful and more secure, but at the cost of harming other wizards and the natural environment. The greed of a small percentage of wizards is responsible for poverty, homelessness, pollution, environmental destruction, easily broken consumer goods, hunger, war, and many other devastating things.

Workaholism

Many people are brought up with an emphasis on efficiency and productivity doing work. However, it is important to realize that there are a number of ways to be efficient and productive, and one of those ways involves taking care of yourself. It may seem as though something awful will happen if you take a break from all the work you "need" to do, as if walls will crumble or some other catastrophe will occur, but this is very rarely true. Contentment and happiness become harder to grasp the less you care for yourself, and so it is important to take the time necessary to recharge and enjoy life.

Try scheduling one day a week that is absolutely your day. Plan the entire time around good self-care, and do nothing (even thinking) related to projects or work that have been put upon you. It may be hard at first, but undoing the learned behavior of overworking yourself and instead putting a priority on mental wellness is an important step to finding contentment in life. If one day is too much initially, try for half the day, or an hour each day. Another option is to go on a weekend adventure, or schedule time off for something longer. You deserve it.

As you unravel the spell of workaholism, you may realize how silly it is that you work so hard, or that what you're doing every day isn't actually what you would like to be doing. Listen to these forces and perhaps it will lead you to finding a job where you have to work less, get more time off, or start your own business.

Media

Media is a powerful tool that inspires thoughts, emotions, and experiences we may never have had otherwise. They give us heroes to look up to and allow us to see romanticized or condensed stories of lifestyles we may wish to embrace or strive for. They can also become addictions that cause us to avoid dealing with reality.

Consider the entertainment you voluntarily and involuntarily experience. Are you utilizing media in a destructive manner to make your mood worse? Try going without media for a time to see how the spells it casts are influencing you. I have found that media can be an addiction that perpetuates an avoidance of emotions, thoughts, creativity, and healthy habits. What do you really need to know about? Are you drowning in the darkness of media sensationalism and propaganda when you could be caring for your local community and things you can actually change? Once you realize what is beneficial to you and what is not, add back in those items and be wary of others.

Simultaneously, or instead of removing media from your life, study "media literacy." Studying media will help you understand the underlying messages presented, see biases, and question the authenticity of the information given. From here you can begin removing oppressive and demeaning media from your life, and substitute appropriate alternatives in their place.

Remember that media is missing key components of the original event. The original event experienced in person will almost always be able to impact you in a deeper way because it is more immersive and requires more of your time and energy, so engage in media's true form whenever possible. Go see live music, an author question and answer session, workshops, or even actors performing and doing retakes on a set. By only witnessing the recorded version of media, you miss out on the unique stories experienced in person surrounded by creators and their audience.

Judgment of Good and Bad

Judgment is natural, and some judgments are important. We like some things and we dislike others, and speed up our decisions by applying experiences we've had before to similar experiences in the future. In a world with so much to judge though, judgments make us spend more time than we likely want thinking negatively, and in turn drive us into sadness, anger, and depression. Not only that, but judgments make communication and conflict resolution almost impossible, because they hide feelings and needs. Statements such as "that is good" or "that is bad" give an individual little information about how to proceed with a situation. This is especially the case when we dwell on our judgments and carry them around with us.

Reworking judgments begins with becoming aware of these destructive spells. The feelings created when we judge are almost instantaneous, so it is difficult to notice that the judgmental thoughts and the associated feelings are in fact separate. If you remove the judgments, the feelings will not arise. Judgment can be quite subtle, such as when reading a book written in a way you dislike, or more overbearing, such as when you see someone dressed in a way you've always associated with something bad.

What do you lose by dropping your judgments of things or people? Probably nothing. What do you gain? A lot more opportunities for happiness and to experience the world. Here are some tips for dropping judgment:

- Try for one day to not judge anyone; to genuinely live in the present moment without criticisms in order to give everyone a fair try. Don't complain or vent about anything.

- Check your ego. Everyone has something they are equally talented at as you are, and everyone has to start somewhere. Don't make assumptions about the capabilities of a person based on appearance or first impressions. Everyone has had different opportunities and experiences in life to get to where they are now.

- Realize that no judgments or notions of good and evil are universal. Rather they are flexible and ever-changing concepts that make up part of a wizard clan's culture.

- Practice mindfulness meditation. Instead of thinking about your environment, fully experience the sensations created by that environment and your own body.

- When you judge, move on without dwelling on the thoughts or holding onto the associated feelings.

- Challenge yourself to do the opposite of what your reactionary judgment tells you to do.

- When you experience anger towards a person, acknowledge your feelings to be the result of unmet needs you personally have rather than the actions of the other person. See NONVIOLENT COMMUNICATION under POWERING UP YOUR WORDS.

Invisible Stresses

All wizards experience invisible stresses, things that are so inherently part of one's life that it is hard to realize the negative impact. These include things like ugly buildings, barking dogs, strangers, cars, and loneliness. Invisible stresses are especially detrimental to emotionally sensitive wizards. You have some control over these influences, but many are dictated by the wizards in control.

Believing Humans are Separate from Nature

Modern civilization largely disconnects people from nature and the resources used to build our society. Part of the problem is that even though most humans now utilize resources from all over the world, they are only capable of having a localized sense of perception. This means that it is hard for people to see their responsibility in a forest being clearcut for wood and farmland, or a mountain being blown apart for metals, or rivers being overfished, or slave labor being used to make goods. Instead, you go into a store and buy a product with no awareness of the dozens of people who helped in the process or the raw resources used in the making of it.

You are a part of nature, and the collective stresses that humans are putting on the natural world is negatively impacting all life on Earth. The problem is so dire that some scientists speculate that without a radical change in our consumption of goods and use of energy, humans will be extinct well before the end of the century. While this problem is a collective one, there are also some more responsible than others. These most notably include the wizards in control such as politicians, business owners, and religious leaders.

The Wizards in Control

You are presently under the influence of many beneficial and destructive spells cast by the leaders of various wizarding clans and collective groups of wizards. Wizards in control use money, political connections, law makers, and propaganda to maintain their stronghold. Most wizards are unaware of these dominate spell influences, which include things like the consumption of media, fashion trends, politics, religious practices, and what you think about.

Even if one does attempt to weave in their own spells of truth, rarely is it that their power will be successful against a wizarding clan's prevailing spells. This is because each member of that clan is continuously recasting spells on themselves and each other to preserve the spell's power, sometimes intentionally, but often without thinking. As these clans have much greater magic potential and spell casting abilities than an individual, it is difficult for new ideas to overtake long established ones.

The most potent spells today are cast by nations, political and religious leaders, entertainment and news media, corporations, and big businesses. These clans usually derive great power from spells cast by wizards long since deceased. Take for instance thousands of years old beliefs, the design of various tools, the words which comprise the English language, dating rituals, the fictional characters which are discussed in daily conversation, or the associations made with different colors.

Many wizarding leaders work to prevent free thinking and block common wizards from obtaining their highest forms. It is therefore imperative to be aware of the magical influences manipulating how you exist, and work on dismantling them from your behaviors, thinking, and wizarding clan. While difficult, it is quite possible to change existing wizard clans, create new ways for people to think, or even overthrow the wizards in control. You can learn how to use these types of spells in MAGIC ALCHEMY as well as undo destructive behaviors in yourself with many of the other spells outlined throughout this book.

The Possible World

In large part because of the wizards in control, most common wizards do not realize what a healthy and thriving civilization can look like, let alone that one is possible for everyone. Most nations, but especially industrialized ones, are entrenched in a number of problems, including:

- Economic disparity

- Pollution

- Obsession with acquiring more material goods and money

- Lack of community causing a deep sense of loneliness

- Overpopulation

- Conflict and war

- Car-centric culture in which most public space is consumed by roads and traffic, making walking or cycling stressful if not impossible as well as limiting the amount of plants and biodiversity in an area

- Media addiction

- Disconnection from where food comes from

A healthy culture might have some of the following aspects:

- Filled with plants and nature, including parks, large preserved wilderness areas, and greenery in between sidewalks and streets

- Local production of food and goods

- Education that teaches healthy communication, dealing with conflict, getting into successful relationships, creativity, and handling finances

- Women feel safe expressing themselves, can take on whichever careers they desire, and do not fear being sexually harassed in public

- Men feel comfortable expressing their emotions and communicating directly in non-aggressive ways

- A person's biological sex does not dictate how they act, dress, or make decisions

- News reports primarily focus on positive and uplifting events

- Public spaces which can easily be used by any social demographic for a variety of purposes

- Tenant rights such as banning no-cause evictions and limiting rent increases

- Voting systems that accurately represent a population's voice such as Score Then Automatic Runoff (STAR) or Ranked Choice Voting (RCV)

- Provide support services such as free housing and counseling for people suffering from mental instability, homelessness, abuse, or other struggles

- Universal healthcare

- Water, housing, food, and contraception are basic rights guaranteed to a nation's citizens

- Rehabilitation services are used rather than punishment for people convicted of crimes

- Focus on communal living in which residents share supplies, food, and work tasks like cooking and cleaning

- Law enforcement agents use mediation and non-lethal weapons to deescalate a situation

- Guaranteeing a basic income, especially in competitive economic systems that rely on a number of people being unemployed

- The health of a nation is based on its general happiness rather than economic output

- Support of the arts through education, public artworks, and museums

- Banning corporations and promoting small businesses and worker-owned collectives

- Sustainable energy resources and generally designing society to use less energy by creating well-insulated homes, public transit systems, and growing food locally

- Preference for beauty over efficiency in design, especially in the architecture of homes and businesses

- Designing cities to be walked and cycled in rather than driven around

Introducing changes like these to a civilization or culture are crucial for combating the darkness (see COPING WITH THE DARKNESS) and helping people reach their highest forms (see A WIZARD'S HIGHEST FORM). Even if you are given everything in this world you want, there will still be pain and discomfort in your life, and others will still be without. It is therefore your duty to use your privileges to help others. You can read about how to empower your whole wizard clan into a more uplifting environment in MAGIC ALCHEMY.

. . .

Life Mapping

What destructive spells are you under and how did you fall under their effect? What is their source and how can you work to undo them?

MAGIC ALCHEMY

*A*lchemy is the process of transformation. Consciously or unconsciously, wizards alter the meaning and effects of magic over time. Between different wizard clans, individuals, and wizarding nations, the same word, motion, feeling, thought, magic object, and so on may have a considerably different effect. Not only can one spell be replaced by another to create the same effect, a magic spell may also be redefined to create an entirely new effect. Alchemy is essential in transforming destructive spells in yourself, your peers, and in the broader wizarding world.

The flexibility and vast diversity of spells throughout the world has huge implications on all wizards—it means that anyone can define their personal reality as well as redefine a wizard clan's culture and way of being. Unlike the limitations in using alchemy to transform physical objects, magic alchemy is capable of transforming any spell into another when the proper technique is used.

Alchemizing Your Personal Magic

As you become aware of the spells you consciously and unconsciously cast out of habit, you may realize that a number of those spells are detrimental to your wizardly powers. Fortunately, undesirable spells may be transmuted into useful alternatives through reforming habits (see HABITS AND AUTOCASTING MAGIC SPELLS under CONTROLLING YOUR MAGIC), the subconscious (see ALTERING SUBCONSCIOUS BEHAVIORS under THE

SUBCONSCIOUS), and a type of magic alchemy known to wizard psychologists as "cognitive restructuring." Cognitive restructuring is useful for sorting out rational thoughts from distorted ones. Common distortions include:

- Thinking if you haven't reached perfection then you're a failure.

- Making generalizations such as stereotyping a race of people as all believing the same thing.

- Filtering out everything but the negative in a situation.

- Always needing to be right and not listening to others' reasoning.

- Making conclusions without substantial evidence.

- Magnifying things out of proportion or minimizing their significance.

- Making conclusions through your emotions rather than objective reasoning.

- Confusing what you should do with what you must do.

- Believing everything that people say and do is a judgment on you.

- Blaming other people for your emotional state.

You can untangle distorted thinking by sorting out which thoughts and feelings are true and justified, and which need alteration. Maybe you're feeling angry about a conversation you had, or sad and anxious because of a breakup. On a piece of paper list the feelings you're experiencing and the thoughts and beliefs that are arising. Think about each of these thoughts rationally. List those distortions beside each thought. You can now start writing out alternative thoughts that more accurately describe the objective truth.

Activism and Alchemizing the Magic of Other Wizards

Perhaps you want your wizard clan to believe in a new idea or concept, perhaps you want more rights given to a certain demographic you belong to, or perhaps you want to completely eradicate certain magic spells from a wizard clan's usage. Maybe you will even make it your mission to educate the masses about magic. These processes are possible through alchemizing the magic of your own wizard clan, or that of a wizard clan you do not belong to. In common nomenclature, an alchemist who attempts to change magic spells on a political or social level is known as an activist, though may also be known as an advocate or volunteer. There are many methods of being an effective activist. This can be a time consuming process, in the realm of decades or even centuries, but there are many methodologies to magic alchemy, some faster than others.

The basics of activist alchemy

Being an activist is a fulfilling art that takes the knowledge and skill of many magic spells, and typically the forces of many wizards banded together in a common cause. Take time to understand the wizard you are trying to change and what motivates them to cast particular spells. You will also benefit from understanding the historical context of where a spell arose from, so do your magical research! You don't need the whole clan to adopt a belief, but if you can get a percentage of the population to take on your ideas, then it will spread through popular culture and take root in younger generations.

An individual can be extraordinarily powerful in creating change, but groups are necessary to alchemizing the spells of an entire wizard clan. Gather people together who share your passionate resolve for change. An alchemist group is a community as described in MAGICAL ALLIES, and can be fostered in the same way. The only major difference is that often alchemist groups have much more ideological diversity than most stable communities do. Beyond being banded together in the name of a social or environmental cause, many activists within a group have diverging viewpoints on religion, spirituality, politics, food, the environment, gender, and so forth. This is great for generating ideas and having a wide network, but can also lead to a lot of conflict, slowed progress, or even destroy the group altogether. You need numbers, but know when a member is scaring off new recruits, creating a toxic atmosphere, or preventing you from achieving your goals.

As you enter into this process, know that notions of good and evil are different to each wizard clan and individual—there is no universal standard. Your goal as an activist is in fact to spread your own beliefs through either transformation or destruction of those ideas you think poorly of. Your concept of good and evil can be useful as a rallying point to people who support your beliefs, but it is a terrible way to try convincing someone else that you are right to alchemize or destroy their magic spells simply by touting notions of what is good and evil or right and wrong.

Activist alchemy

There are many methods of alchemizing the spells of a group of wizards, each effective or useful in its own way. These include:

- Non-Violent Direct Action: Usually takes the form of disrupting an event, either by causing a ruckus through singing and shouting, or by blockading passageway to an event. Outright defiance of the dominant culture also works, such as when wizard Rosa Parks refused to give up her seat on a bus in opposition to segregation laws.

- Violent Direct Action: Using forceful or destructive means to make a statement or attempt to create change, most often employed by wizard militaries. These include setting property on fire, violence, assassination, riots, torture, and even computer hacking.

- Hacking and Programming: With many wizards relying on robots for their survival now, those with knowledge of how to create and manipulate the world of electronic devices and data networks have incredible power to both destroy and create.

- Indirect Action: Shows how meaningful a cause is to a person, such as with hunger strikes or signing a petition online. Typically these have little influence on anything other than as a means of drawing attention to an activist cause and potentially gathering new allies.

- Education: Educating a populace about a topic they were previously unaware of via fliers, presentations, art, conversations, videos, etc.

- Idea Exposure: Introducing a diversity of beliefs is responsible for changing many magic spells over time. When ideologically different people live in close proximity or have access to each other through things like the internet, many are forced to question their beliefs. On the flip side, if a group of people secludes themselves from outside ideas, their beliefs can exist unchallenged, though they may not grow as they would in a diverse setting.

- Communication: Casually talk to people about why a particular magic spell is problematic to use, and give them alternatives. Different situations may call for violent or nonviolent communication. Violent communication can work by shaming wizards into not using particular spells, although it is unlikely that they will like you or actually support what you believe. Nonviolent communication is a method of connecting with a person's basic human needs and is much better at creating mutual understanding than swearing or yelling at a person (see NONVIOLENT COMMUNICATION under POWERING UP YOUR WORDS). You could also invite several knowledgeable speakers together to host a community discussion on a subject.

- Youth Education: Since activist alchemy can take a considerable amount of time to transform magic, and adults are often set in their ways, focusing on introducing new magic spells to youth through entertainment, the internet, and public education is the easiest way to alchemize a wizard clan's use of spells.

- Propaganda: This can be done through fliers, news broadcasts, articles, posters, speeches, peer pressure, etc. The best propaganda speaks to a person's basic emotional and material needs, like happiness or money.

- Laws: Creating or demolishing laws is a fairly effective way to alchemize a spell, because following or not following that law is connected to a wizard's basic need for freedom—breaking the law will potentially end their freedom. It also makes everyone aware of the alternatively desired spell, even if they don't really want to use it. While effective, many laws are not well enforced. Some laws can also have the opposite of the desired effect.

- Lawyers: These are very powerful wizards that can help pass new laws, or challenge existing ones and magic spells being cast by certain wizards and businesses. Some lawyers will assist activist wizards for free, but others charge a considerable sum of money.

- Self-Care and Passion: People who take care of themselves, especially within oppressive institutions, can be amazing beacons of light and sources of inspiration for wizards who are lost or do not entirely agree with an existing system. You can show them the amazing world that is possible if things were to change.

- Creation: Alchemy may be accomplished by way of creating things. Many activists just focus on destroying existing institutions before ever having an alternative to fill in or replace what they're opposing. Showing wizards a "better" world that is possible makes convincing them of your ideals much easier.

- Purchases: Enough people opting out of or into buying something can crash or bolster industries and services. This type of alchemy has been used to make businesses close, food stores change ingredients, and products be tested without animals.

- Philosophy: Many philosopher wizards have thought a lot about the meaning of life (or the lack thereof) and, through their written ideas and observations of humanity and existence, come to conclusions that whole wizard clans may decide to follow.

- Scientific Research: Wizards in recent times have some amount of trust in scientists, using the scientific method and the observable world to understand a concept, or discovering the benefits or drawbacks to a particular set of spells or materials. Scientific research becomes especially helpful when paired with lawyers, law, medical fields, and the engineering of new wizardly equipment.

- Fun and Entertainment: Activism doesn't have to be dull and stressful. It can involve making educational games for children, creating art, performing a theatrical act, singing a song, making people laugh, dressing up in costume, and generally uplifting the lives of others. Activists that incorporate these aspects into their causes are much less likely to burn out while drawing a greater number of members to their ranks.

- Donations: Activists always need more money, more volunteers, more food, and more supplies. Donating is a positive way to alchemize what you have to help someone else.

- Creating Small-Scale Examples: Even if your community or city is just a few thousand people, you can exemplify systems to show the world what is possible. Generally larger communities want data and examples before adopting change, so your local actions could start a mass movement. Consider this with voting systems, technologies, community gardens, vertical farms, re-imagined prisons, and other reforms.

- Community building: Communities help people end their roles in individualism and tend to be a much healthier way to go about existing.

On being an effective activist

So you have an alchemist group and have decided on a technique to use for transforming the magic spells of a culture. Now you need to make sure the collective stays healthy, your actions are worthwhile, and everything doesn't fall apart.

Choosing a goal that creates change

Many groups choose goals that feel like they create change, but in the long run do very little toward fixing the source of a problem. Understand the systems in place that support the existence of a particular magic spell. Where is the root cause, and how can you address that? Too often activist groups blame common people or an individual's purchasing decisions when in fact it is the government, culture, business practices, or a law. For instance, before you blame someone for the consumer product they are buying, think about the bigger picture about why that product exists and what systems are in place which are causing the individual to buy it.

Some forms of activism can also be split into actions that feel good on an ethical or spiritual level, and actions that work to create broader change. Many potential change-makers feel they are being effective by only doing things that personally feel good. You have to understand however that the wizards in control are willing to do almost anything to secure more power and dictate the lives of you and your loved ones. Wizards who are only willing to take actions which feel good are limited in their ability to create broad change. Taken to an extreme, you could live separated from civilization on your off-grid farm and argue that you are living in harmony with nature, but your ability to influence people, politics, and businesses will be extremely limited. In other words, you could be 100% sustainable, or you could help a city full of people each be 1% more sustainable.

You need to be practical with the dollars you are spending and the activities you are bringing into or cutting out of your life. Is not owning a car going to destroy the automotive industry in the United States where there is dreadful public transit or is it just going to slow down your ability to take action? Think bigger. Direct your activism at what is effective and allows you to do more. How can you create direct and large-scale change? What do people need? Remember that you are a culture trying to spread your beliefs by transforming or destroying other cultures. Don't try to sugar-coat it, how can you do this effectively?

Educating yourself and new members

Educate new members on the subtleties of magic, how the particular magic spell you are trying to alchemize has come into being, and how the wizards who use that spell function psychologically in communication and mannerisms. Some activists are inspired to join movements out of pure anger or passion, and do not understand much about the cause or how to effectively alchemize magic spells. Suggest that new members:

- Look at examples of effective activists throughout history.

- Know how much time they can devote to being an activist and how much time they are going to reserve for self-care.

- Have a supportive community that does not involve campaign work, or at least does not always talk about it. Life is more than just work and intense conversations!

Toxic people

Mediate with, remove, or refuse entry to members who exhibit toxic behaviors without a desire to change. Just because a person is passionate about the same things as your group is doesn't actually mean they're going to help you.

Security culture

If your cause is at risk of being accused of wrong doings or attacked for its beliefs, you must be careful about what your opponents hear and see of you. Apply security techniques and be careful about who you share information with. Of course, if you belong to certain institutions you may have enough resources to defend yourself or strike fear in those who would oppose your alchemy, but typically only governments, militarized groups, and religious organizations have this sort of power.

Cost, care, and convenience

Many activist campaigns struggle because the framing of their mission is not in line with what potential supporters want, need, or believe. People are especially interested in saving money, saving time, and more strongly meeting their basic needs and desires.

- Money: Does this product cost less than another? Will this lower taxes?

- Time: Is this activity convenient and easy to sign up for? Does the location of this business help people access XYZ thing faster?

- Care: Does this line up with a person's basic needs and beliefs about the world? Does it give them better access to food or make them healthier? Does it speak to their religious, spiritual, moral, or ethical views?

If you can center your message around at least two of these, then it makes your campaign relatable to a wider audience—people don't care about what you're saying unless it directly impacts them in some way.

Bias

Many activist groups are ineffective because they forget that their opponents belong to a completely separate reality, truth, and order of magic spells. Wizards are often selfish when dealing with strangers. They care a whole lot about themselves, their friends, and their family, and not a whole lot about you and your movement. This is why it is essential that while trying to convince a person to support your movement you connect it to their wants, needs, and emotional values in some way. How does your cause impact them? Wizards tend to stick to particular media channels that may not be friendly to your beliefs, so you'll need to figure out ways of spreading information to these people through other channels such as fliers, banners, art, television commercials, one-on-one conversations, and the internet.

Audience

Keep in mind what attracts people the most. You may host a party or benefit show for a cause, but know that highlighting the music will bring in more people than if you just focus on the cause. Unless your activist group or cause is popular already, most people won't attend or pay attention. Wizards love fun and play. Draw them in with incentives they care about like social interaction, drinking, dancing, laughter, good music, food, education, entertainment, and the like.

Use the appropriate conversation style

Different types of communication are better at different times. Is violent communication worthwhile? Will non-violent communication reach a person? Is keeping silent the better choice? Each is useful in its own way. For instance, violent communication, such as yelling at a person, may be necessary if you have a limited time to convey information, but in the wrong space may also put your personal safety at risk. Some marginalized groups start off by using a lot of violent communication as a means of expressing their existence, intolerance of certain magic spells, and that retaliation is to be expected. Nonviolent communication can be used to de-escalate violent situations and is a great method of emotionally connecting with people in a relatable way. It is especially good for communicating to allies of your cause or people who you know are open minded to it.

Tips on making information memorable

- New knowledge sticks best to already existing knowledge. When presenting information, relate it to commonly known concepts, beliefs, pop-culture, or images. This is why metaphors are extremely powerful!

- The brain remembers sexual, weird, and humorous information better than it does other types.

- As mentioned in TYPES OF WIZARDS, different people learn better with different senses, so do your best to educate others on a subject using a variety of means.

- Tell people or yourself to do instead of not to do. For instance, "please be quiet" instead of "don't play music," or "I will eat more rice" instead of "I won't eat bread." Using the actionable word you want a person to avoid doing can cause confusion or make the person want to do that thing anyways. Using positive phrasing also gives an alternative to pursue.

- Mystery can be used to perk interest, such as "click here to find out what happens next!" or cutting off a sentence early so that the reader will want to finish and must click through to see.

It's okay to be a hypocrite

No one is perfect, and in today's globalized world, almost anything you do will be hurtful to someone or something. Depriving yourself of everything that causes suffering in the world will prevent you from working effectively or having as great of a reach. Just do what you can and know that taking care of your basic needs and striving for happiness is perfectly okay.

Balance your time

The most important thing to consider during times of difficulty in an advocacy, volunteer, or activist group is that even the smallest accomplishment is moving towards positive results. Changing the status quo may take decades, so remind yourself that success is possible by watching or reading about previous campaigns, or by speaking to older peers within your movement. Consider the amount of work you personally take on to reach a given goal. Are you doing more than you can handle?

It's easy to believe that everything will collapse if you reduce the amount of work you do, but the more long-term you can work, the better. Why not take actions that are more manageable, or recruit new members? Working on small goals that show immediate results provides mental rewards that boost personal and group wellness. Ensuring needs are met to create a group of well-rested and positive people may also make it easier to recruit new members.

It is important to realize that as an activist, one is not living the life they would be living if the world fit their desires. What would you be doing if you were not doing activist work? It is important to occasionally live that life, or incorporate parts of it into your downtime. It is also okay to stop and take a rest if things get too stressful. Know your limitations and establish them with your peers. Pass the work on when you reach that limit, because it is better to say "no" to new tasks than it is to become overwhelmed, ignore your personal health, and never return to the group.

Maintain your mental health

While attempting to make society and the world into a better place brings a great amount of meaning and fulfillment to one's life, it can also be a harrowing process. It often means dealing with guilt, anger, verbal abuse, cultural deprivation, as well as anxiety as you attempt to create change against enormous resistance. These factors can trigger depression or depressed feelings and lead to burnout and dropping out of your cause. With this knowledge it is up to you to change the culture surrounding your activism, to step back from it, or balance it with other mentally healthy activities. More than anything, just remember that you are important too and that a content and happy mind is much more effective at creating positive change.

How to present yourself

Activists may carry an identity that is at odds with the mainstream identity. This difference in culture can create a level of disapproval between parties which immediately weakens your argument. As much as many people may not like it, your appearance and choice of words are both part of your argument spell. Be sure that when making an argument for your cause, you are communicating in respect to the other party's cultural identity. Some people simply should not be a spokesperson for a group, and some words and images should simply not be used when spreading information.

Part of a person receiving information you impart to them is that person's ability to listen to and relate to what is being said. Divisions do exist in this world. If you have a mohawk and are wearing a tutu, you probably won't have good communication with a politician in a business suit. People feel more comfortable and trusting of wizards who they can relate to and feel similar with ideologically, so put on your best act.

Creating media

The most important factor in making information aesthetically pleasing and effective is time. Take it slow. If possible, have someone with an art background work on the aesthetic parts, or at least give you pointers. Always have someone else familiar with the group or event double check and critique your work. Don't be offended if they tell you to redo it or to hand the project over to someone else. It can also be a good idea to look at other pieces of media you find appealing. Get inspired, or even copy the basic design. This is a great way to learn what works and what doesn't, especially when trying to make media accessible to your audience. There is also a lot of free software available for creating images, fliers, documents, audio, and videos with, so you should be able to make something decent regardless of having financial resources.

Questions to ask yourself with media:

- Is it visibly eye-catching even at a distance?

- Is there a good balance of text to images?

- Do the images used provide information to the viewer or resonate with the audience's interests and culture?

- Are there any assumptions about the audience made?

- If there is a sound component, can you hear everything being said clearly?

- What audience does the media correspond with?

- If you are trying to get people to do something, are there positive incentives for them to do it?

- Does the media conjure emotions? Excitement? Sadness? Hardship? Happiness?

Learning styles and presentations

Not all people learn best in the same way. Many prefer an auditory, visual, or kinesthetic approach to receiving information. A truly effective presentation will appease all three learning styles through narrative, visuals, and hands-on activities.

- Auditory (hear): A good public speaker uses their voice and memory effectively. They memorize part of, if not all their speech. Be familiar with the information you are going to present. Alternate the emotions and vocal tones you present to listeners as well. Information is generally best presented in ways that the audience is shown something instead of having it logically explained to them, so use metaphors, stories, and humor when possible.

- Visual (see): To appease visual learners create signs, handouts, powerpoint presentations, or even just an outline of your talking points. Use hand and facial gestures, and have paper and pencils available for people to take notes.

- Kinesthetic (touch): Make your speech "hands-on" by asking your audience questions, allowing them to ask you questions throughout the presentation, breaking into groups for discussion, or by playing a game.

Communication

It is essential that all activists learn different styles of communication to handle situations appropriately. Many of us were never taught how to communicate, but just pieced together what we could from growing up in our communities and the media we ingested, without understanding the nuances of tone, word choice, rhythm, and so forth. Here are some general suggestions for communicating as an activist:

- Try your best to call people in, not out. Or in other words, have a conversation with people instead of communicating aggressively.

- A person who enters into an argument with you or makes statements with anger or violence often must first be mediated with to listen to your side. Your goal is to calm them down by openly listening to their needs without reacting in argument, criticism, or judgment. Ask questions. You can state your side once they have calmed down and moved from the emotional to rational side of thought.

- Have empathy.

- Use positive reinforcement. Positive reinforcement is more effective than negative reinforcement because rewarding a person gives them a reason to exhibit a new behavior, whereas punishing someone for a bad behavior does nothing toward showing them an alternative.

- Those who ignore or mock your desire for change may not be willing to alter their behaviors. It may be best to not waste your time on these individuals.

- If you are trying to make someone listen to you, find some things that you agree about first before getting into contentious topics. Essentially you want to establish trust and even friendship before any negative talk.

Arguing and logical fallacies

When arguing with a person you want a solid case that your opponent's demographic can understand and connect with on some level. Many statements, known as "logical fallacies," can weaken an argument or diminish its agreeability. These include things like making assumptions or using information that does not actually correlate to your final conclusion. Seek out online resources and grimoires for a complete list.

Privilege and guilt

Many activists experience guilt regarding their lifestyle or position of privilege, especially from the blame they receive from other activists. If you are called out as oppressive by someone, it is okay. Apologize, listen, and try to ask questions if it is not apparent why the thing said was offensive. Do your own research to become informed on the type of oppression.

That being said, what one person, group, or culture thinks is offensive or oppressive changes depending on the person, group, or culture being interacted with. Do your best not to be oppressive or offensive, but realize that you will need to change your language and actions depending on who you are around. That is why asking questions and not making assumptions is so important while interacting with others. Note that it is impossible and unhealthy to attempt to please everyone at all times. You can only do the best that you can do and sometimes that means learning through mistakes.

In general you don't need to have guilt about who you are, even if that means indulging in mainstream culture or your personal privileges. No matter how you go about it, partaking in industrialized civilization directly or indirectly oppresses a human being or other living entity. Even so, working within systems of oppression generally allows you to create much more positive change than if you separated yourself from civilization and were "completely" anti-oppressive.

Blame and oppressive anti-oppression

Some activists live with a lot of blame and hatred of the lifestyles and privileges of others. People who spread the teachings of anti-oppression with these feelings sometimes fall into oppressive behaviors themselves. This group is one of the greatest internal challenges activists face today because while well-meaning, they often make activist circles into alienating, offensive, exclusive, ineffective, negative, or triggering spaces. They should be mediated with or removed from the group to help maintain mental wellness, effectiveness, and positivity. These people are marked by their violent communication, categorization of ignorance as oppressive, ignoring their personal privileges, and dismissing the validity of a person's cultural identity. Allies should be especially careful with how they inform others because they are speaking for another person or group of people.

Breaking away from "us" versus "them"

Most everyone is trying to get by and has the same basic needs, no matter what their upbringing. Relating your vision of the world to those basic needs is one of the most powerful ways of speaking to any culture or sort of person. Instead of generalizing a group of people, speak one-on-one with individuals who do not meet your personal needs with nonviolent communication (see POWERING UP YOUR WORDS). Challenge yourself to have empathy before you express anger, and think about what unmet needs you and the person you are communicating with have before speaking. Most of all, avoid creating stereotypes for groups. It only alienates people from one another and reinforces those behaviors!

Make it fun

Be sure that you are including humor, silliness, and social downtime with your work. Positivity and love are the most powerful tools activists can use to fight for their causes. They not only help draw new people in but also prevent burnout for existing members. Consider celebrating the things that are important to you, playing games, or making your informational materials especially artful and full of humor. With meetings, start off with a silly check-in question. Bring the community together with child-friendly potlucks and educational games. Most activist groups are small enough that you have a lot of power to enact change, so do your best to alter the mundane status quo.

Creating a mass movement

In order to overthrow any of the wizards and clans in control spreading darkness throughout the earth, you have to build a mass movement. Individuals can make great leaders, but it is only with their followers that they have power—and you need a lot of power to take on those in control. It should be noted that mass movements can consume a great amount of time to build and many are crushed by the wizards in control using propaganda or law enforcement. Many others however have succeeded or at the very least introduced powerful ideas to the mainstream which can then be spread further. This is especially true for movements that focus on influencing children and teenagers with developing brains rather than old wizards.

Most mass movements appeal to a large population, have scientific or moral backing, find support from some of the wizards in control, can secure a large amount of funding, effectively use news and social media outlets to spread information, improve a group's access to their basic needs, and generally make the human life better. Successful movements will employ some of the techniques used by the wizards in control and often will have to focus on making small changes rather than ones which would completely transform how a culture functions. In nations with powerful law enforcement bodies, non-violent movements tend to be more effective. You can learn more by reading about movements such as black rights, Occupy, feminism, Arab Spring, counterculture, cooperatives, socialism, communism, and environmentalism.

Often artists will be the first to introduce a movement to a mainstream population through things like books, fictional stories, songs, poems, paintings, workshops, and theater. Mass movements can gain great sway if depicted in mainstream television productions or spoken about by famous musicians. This is often more effective by showing instead of telling an audience about a cause. The goal is to normalize an idea to the extent that people start asking "why isn't it like this everywhere?" Using subtlety and slowly introducing a concept helps prevent an audience from putting up defensive spells which would otherwise block an idea from becoming part of their reality. That said, shock value and fear can also work if an audience already cares about a cause but is simply unaware of it—this is typically the case when it relates broadly to the viewers' basic needs, for instance in the case of environmental concerns.

A spell to save the world

Wizards all over the Earth are working hard at alchemizing the destructive spells which not only make life less enjoyable, but also threaten its very existence. This is a difficult task with the wizards in control maintaining power over the masses. What is needed is a spell which connects people together in such a way that it takes power away from the ruling wizards. One method of accomplishing this feat is by sharing more, buying less, building communities, and localizing economies. The more self-sufficient areas are and the more citizens work together, the better.

The most essential aspect of unifying people together is creating a desirable incentive that transcends a person's beliefs. Being nourished, having fun, making friends, and saving money are things that all people want dearly. What spells can you weave to save the environment? The people? The world?

Business

Many of the same activist techniques can be used to alchemize your time into wealth by starting a business. Wealth can take many forms, but most businesses derive money from their efforts. Money is a symbolic representation of almost any material item and can also help in manifesting certain emotional qualities. Money however is not a good driving force behind a business—a business must address a need or want that people have. Perhaps that is to be entertained, to be healed, to learn job skills, to eat, and so forth. In this way businesses can improve a person and a city's well-being. Creative businesses that act as community hubs can even provide a sense for why a person lives in an area.

Owning a personal businesses is a fulfilling way to find freedom in how you use your time and earn a living. There are many structures for a business and specific laws to follow for each type. In general though, businesses can be an individual effort, a boss with employees, a committee that makes decisions for the employees, or a cooperative in which all employees make decisions together. Businesses can also be primarily focused on earning money or providing some service to the world. If you'd like trying to start your own business:

- Consider what people want or need in your area.

- Choose a specific demographic to sell to. Especially when competing with other businesses, identify a niche market and focus your marketing on them.

- Keep up to date on the latest marketing strategies, most of which are changing all the time.

- Be sure that whatever main sensation that your marketing engages is a quality one—make visuals aesthetically pleasing, make smells aromatic, make audio audible in recordings, etc.

- Marketing is best done by showing instead of telling; in other words, don't tell a person they'll enjoy a product, show someone using the product and enjoying life.

- You'll notice that some marketing focuses on creating an emotional quality in a person, often humorous or sexual in nature. These strategies are attaching a positive emotion to that product or brand when encountered later, increasing the likelihood of engagement by potential customers. Ads also frequently play on guilt or shock value.

- No matter what you're selling, buyers will always appreciate a good experience—make the product worthwhile, use aesthetically pleasing design with the product and packaging, have good customer service protocols, be nice, and give the customer free things or coupons with each purchase.

- Seek out organizations in your town that help with business start-ups either with funding, counseling, networking, or workshops. If these groups do not exist, your county or state business department should be able to help as well if you call them.

- Funding for a new business can come from a great number of places, including bank loans, personal micro-loans, crowd sourcing funds online, grants, hosting benefit shows, or simply working another job.

- Share your story and the authentic reason why your business exists. Stories bring a sense of humanity back into money-making enterprises and is another way to help people connect emotionally to your product. In a competitive marketplace, your story is often the only unique thing that your business has to make itself stand out.

Money doesn't have to be the primary output of a business. For instance, directly trading goods and services through bartering supersedes monetary needs. An hour exchange works by people trading their skills for an hour at a time for another wizard's skills. A business can also pursue a social cause under the direction of a non-profit, but these can still involve quite a lot of monetary earnings.

People can also perform most of the functions that businesses provide for free just for the sake of feeling good about offering a basic human need or building community. This is more easily accomplished as a community, family, or other group structure, but people can offer services, grow food, educate others, share tools, provide housing, have an event space, and so much more, free to the public.

•   •   •

Life Mapping

What aspects of yourself or others do you want to alchemize? How will you go about it? What is an alchemist group you feel drawn to?

THE END OF
WIZARDS

Memories, personalities, individuals, communities, wizard clans, wizard nations, and you will all one day cease to exist. These things are impermanent, and death, at an ideological and physical level, is inevitable. These are not events that necessitate mourning, but rather understanding and cherishing the natural rhythms of being alive, living on Earth, and existing in this universe. Even though death is certain, there is no way of knowing when it will come. Someone with a deathly illness may recover, and another person having an absolutely wonderful day may drop dead. That said, there are many actions that may be taken to extend the probable lifespan of individuals, clans, and the whole wizarding race.

Individuals

Any individual may experience the death of their personality, identity, soul, or physical form. Our personalities and identities can die when confronted with great difficulty or we see a need to transform ourselves. The soul comes and goes as we foster or neglect a friendship with our spiritual energy. The physical form we inhabit ages, grows weak, and departs.

On Earth, life is death and death is life. We cycle through these stages just as all organisms do, dissolving into and out of other forms of matter, thought, and energy. When we die, the spells we cast in the world may remain for quite some time, weaving their way through the lives of others. In this way we continue on as ghosts, slipping through the thoughts, emotions, inspirations, and chaotic flows of the universe. No one knows for certain what happens in physical death, but it is a fantastic mystery that everyone will experience when it is their time.

You never know exactly what tomorrow will bring. It could be the greatest day of your life, or it could be your death. Therefore finding contentment and joy in this moment is important. There can be a lot of obstacles in nurturing a life where you can fully appreciate this amazing time that we live in, but it is possible with the right spells found throughout this book. Finding ways to remember your mortality can help inspire you to focus on the good things in life, find forgiveness, see the bigger picture, and realize how small your problems are. You can bring this awareness to yourself by spending time with older wizards, visiting hospitals and cemeteries, participating in religious and spiritual groups, or by being in nature.

Wizard Clans and Nations

Just as individual wizards may die, so can their clans and nations. Most often these collections of wizards are absorbed into larger wizarding communities, but may also disappear altogether through war, globalization, disinterest from youth to continue on with a legacy, disease, resource depletion, and natural forces such as climate change or various powers from outer space. Absorbed groups may maintain some of their group's culture, but also give up parts of it for what the greater majority believes. Wizard clans that have disappeared do often live on through historical records and archaeological discoveries.

The Human Race

It is unlikely for the human race of wizards to live on forever. In the long term of billions of years, a meteor will smash into the planet, the sun will explode, or a black hole will devour Earth. In the more immediate future, climate change will make the planet inhospitable for nearly all life, nuclear war or damaged nuclear power plants may create a toxic wasteland, and artificial intelligence could decide that humans are unworthy of existence. These immediate realities are all preventable, but require wizards like yourself to take action by using your magic to weave a new global culture that is environmentally friendly and uses science and technological power responsibly.

If you want your legacy to continue existing, if you want the plants and animals to keep thriving, if you want the beautiful discoveries and creations of the wizarding world to persevere for many millenniums, you're going to have to take a stand against the wizards who neglect the future. Read more in ACTIVISM AND ALCHEMIZING THE MAGIC OF OTHER WIZARDS under MAGIC ALCHEMY.

• • •

Life Mapping

What do you want to do with this life that you have been gifted? How can you prepare for death mentally, physically, and spiritually? What holds you back from accepting death as a part of life? How can you help keep the human race alive and thriving for generations to come?

LIFE MAPPING

Throughout *You Are A Great And Powerful Wizard* you will have found questions at the end of each chapter, as well as in A WIZARD'S HIGHEST FORM. If you answered them, these questions will have reflected a great amount about who you are and who you want to become. In this final section you will find a way of synthesizing this information into a more usable form, your life map. With it you will be able to easily see the powers you have available to you, as well as the quests you must embark on to obtain new spells, magical equipment, allies, and your highest form. Some of the questions are repeated from earlier in the book, and others are new.

The life map starts with your current form, comprised of your conscious and subconscious personalities. This gives you a starting point to observe yourself from. Following this we look into where you want to get to, or your highest form. The final series of questions is a deep inquiry into how to get your current form to your highest form, or the alchemizing step. Remember that this can be a lifelong process, and there may be more than just internal factors blocking your way, such as cultural norms, family, laws, and the wizards in control. It is therefore important to be practical in transforming yourself—you may have to join with others working toward transforming dominant wizarding cultures in order to fully realize your highest form.

Your Conscious Form

What is your wizard type? What magical activities and hobbies do you partake in? Who are your human and non-human allies? Who are your human and non-human enemies? What magical objects do you possess? Which spells are you adept at using? How do you cope with the darkness? What types of movement, energy, language, and thought spells do you cast? What magic potions do you consume and how do they impact you? Which wizarding clans and communities do you belong to? What quests are you currently on and which would you like to begin?

Your Subconscious Form

What is the appearance of your shadow and light forms? What do you dream about in your sleep? What things increase your potential of being consumed by forms of the darkness? What things trigger the darkness to consume you? What experiences have trapped emotional energy within you? What self-destructive or negative habits do you have? Which destructive spells are you under the influence of? What addictions do you have? What negative assumptions do you have about yourself? What makes you laugh and smile? What sort of emotions come out in your artwork? What makes you experience love? What are you physically attracted to?

Your Highest Form

In considering the questions below, remember that the following inquiry will help you think about what your highest form might look like: What have you always wanted to do? Who do you look up to? What experiences in your life have made you the happiest? Who would you be if you didn't have to worry about money? What are you capable of when absolutely confident in words and actions? What are you passionate about to the core of your being? What would you do if all your conflicts were settled?

You can further explore your highest form by answering the questions for your conscious and subconscious forms again, but applied to the person you would like to be in the future.

Alchemizing Your Forms

As you finish answering these questions, you can begin to ask yourself the steps needed to embark on a quest to obtain your highest form. What spells need to be alchemized into new forms? What habits do you need to form or deform? What magical equipment do you need? What wizarding career or financial assistance do you require? How do you form meaningful connections with wizards who nourish you? How do you integrate yourself into a community? What systems of oppression need to be ended? Which wizards need to be removed from power? What is your relationship with your shadow and light forms? How do your shadow and light forms benefit you? How do you cope with the darkness?

Remember that this is a lifelong process, and that your highest form may only come out around particular wizards or under specific circumstances. This life map will also change quite a lot as you have new experiences and meet new people. Keep at it, one day at a time. Working toward your highest form will often help others awaken to their full potential as well, so know that the benefits exist beyond yourself.

YOU ARE A GREAT AND POWERFUL WIZARD

You have ample resources for your life's journey, the human experience. It won't always be easy, but having learned the essentials of magic, roadblocks that once seemed insurmountable are manageable possibilities.

While we have covered a great amount of magical knowledge, this book is only the beginning of your magical studies. You have learned how to build communities, change minds, influence cultures, and transform yourself. Perhaps you even discovered the appearance of your highest form or a method to defeat the darkness. What do you want to do with your power?

Every moment, you are capable of so many amazing wonders, and the roads you take from here will determine how you grow and flourish in this lifetime. Wizards will always learn the most through hands-on experience discovered through a willingness to be vulnerable and take a chance. All you need to remember is that you are a great and powerful wizard. Good luck out there on your grand journey through time and space.

WIZARD GLOSSARY

Alchemy: The act of using magic to transform a shape, meaning, emotion, thinking pattern, idea, etc.

The Darkness: Negative or destructive moods which consume a person with things including anxiety, depression, hatred, jealousy, and stereotypes.

Familiar: A non-human organism that you care for and are close friends with.

Grimoire: A book of magic spells.

Highest Form: A wizard's ideal life that they wish to obtain.

Life Map: A guide to who you are now, who you want to become, and how to get there.

Magic: The inherent potential within anything to change reality.

Magic Alchemy: Used to alter the meaning and effects of a particular magic spell.

Magick: In some communities the term magic is associated with performer magicians who use various stage tricks to entertain audiences. Magick is used to differentiate from performance magic and tends to have a spiritual or religious background.

Magic Potential: A person or object's potential to use magic to transform reality and cast particular spells.

Shadow: Your shadow includes all those hidden parts of yourself that you find less than desirable like your judgments, self-doubts, regrets, hypocritical actions, mistakes, vices, shortcomings, and the other things that may lead to a negative or self-destructive mindset.

Soul: A manifestation of a person's total spiritual energy.

Spell: The specific process and actions (or lack thereof) to use magic to alter reality.

Spell Book: A collection of magic spells and how to cast them.

Spell Casting: The act of using magic to transform reality.

Wizard: A person who transforms reality.

Wizard Clan: A group of wizards connected by language, dress, foods, beliefs, and traditions.

BIBLIOGRAPHY

Amin, Zenab, Turhan Canli, and C. Neill Epperson. "Effect of Estrogen-Serotonin Interactions on Mood and Cognition." *Behavioral and Cognitive Neuroscience Reviews* 4.1 (Mar. 2005): 43-58. *Sage Publications. Behavioral and Cognitive Neuroscience.* Web. 9 Jan. 2015. DOI: 10.1177/1534582305277152

Bao, Ai-Min, et al. "Diurnal rhythm of free estradiol during the menstrual cycle." European Journal of Endocrinology 148 (2003): 227-232. European Journal of Endocrinology. Web. 10 Jan. 2015.

Beck, Taylor. "Estrogen and female anxiety." *Harvard Gazette.* 9 Aug. 2012. Web. 9 Jan. 2014.

Brauser, Deborah. "Psychedelic Drugs May Reduce Symptoms of Depression, Anxiety, and OCD." *MedScape News Today.* 25 Aug 2010. Web. 25 Feb 2012.

Brezsny, Rob. *Pronoia.* Berkeley: North Atlantic Books, 2009. Print.

B.S. Gupta and Uma Gupta. "Caffeine and Behavior." P. 21. 1999. *Google Books.* No Date. Web. 29 March 2012.

Cain, Susan. Quiet. New York: Broadway Paperbacks, 2013. Print.

Cajochen, Christian, et al. "Evidence that the Lunar Cycle Influences Human Sleep." *Current Biology* 23.15 (5 Aug. 2013): 1485-1488. *Cell Press.* Web. 8 Dec. 2014. doi: http://dx.doi.org/10.1016/j.cub.2013.06.029

"Carbon Dioxide." *Wisconsin Department of Health Services.* 7 Aug. 2013. Web. 27 Aug 2013.

Carrillo, J.A., and J. Benitez. "Clinically Significant Pharmacokinetic Interactions Between Dietary Caffeine And Medications." *Clinical Pharmacokinetics* 39.2 (2000): 127-153. *Academic Search Premier.* Web. 29 Mar. 2012.

Childs E, Hohoff, et al. "Association Between ADORA2A and DRD2 Polymorphisms and Caffeine-Induced Anxiety." *Neuropsychopharmacology* (2008) 33:2791-2800. *National Institute of Health Public Access.* Web. 29 March 2012.

Cloud, John. "Was Timothy Leary Right?" *Time Magazine.* 19 Apr 2007. Web. 25 Feb 2012.

Cohen, M, N Solowij, and V Carr. "Cannabis, Cannabinoids And Schizophrenia: Integration Of The Evidence." *Australian & New Zealand Journal Of Psychiatry* 42.5 (2008): 357-368. *CINAHL with Full Text.* Web. 21 Feb. 2012.

Crowther, Penny. "Vitamin D: Why We Need More Of The Sunshine Vitamin." *Positive Health* 167 (2010): 1. *Alt HealthWatch.* Web. 20 Feb. 2012.

Cuda, Gretchen. "Just Breathe: Body Has A Built-In Stress Reliever." *NPR Books.* 06 Dec. 2010. Web. 28 March 2014.

Degenhardt, L, W Hall, and M Lynskey. "Exploring The Association Between Cannabis Use And Depression." *Addiction* 98.11 (2003): 1493-1504. *CINAHL with Full Text.* Web. 21 Feb. 2012.

Delude, Cathryn M. "Brain researchers explain why old habits die hard." *MIT News.* 19 Oct 2005. Web. 20 Jun 2013.

"Dietary Supplement Fact Sheet: Vitamin D." *Office of Dietary Supplements. National Institutes of Health. USA.gov.* No date. Web. 15 Jul 2012.

Diamond, Jed. "What Your Doctor Won't Tell You about Male Hormonal Cycles." *Goodtherapy.org.* 9 Oct. 2012. Web. 8 Jan. 2015.

European College of Neuropsychopharmacology. "Birth season affects your mood in later life, new research suggests." ScienceDaily. ScienceDaily, 18 October 2014. Web. 7 Jan. 2015.

Evans, Dr. Mike. "23 and 1/2 Hours" Online Video. YouTube. 2 Dec 2011. Web. 20 Feb 2012.

Field T, Diego M, and Hernandez-Reif M. "Moderate pressure is essential for massage therapy effects." *International Journal of Neuroscience* 120.5 (May 2010): 381-385. *US National Library of Medicine.* Web. 23 Sep. 2013. doi: 10.3109/00207450903579475

Field, Tiffany M. "Massage therapy effects." *American Psychologist* 53.12 (Dec. 1998): 1270-1281. Web. 10 Sep. 2013. doi: 10.1037/0003-066X.53.12.1270

Gail C. Farmer, et al. "Alcohol Use And Depression Symptoms Among Employed Men And Women." *American Journal Of Public Health* 77.6 (1987): 704-707. *Academic Search Premier*. Web. 20 Feb. 2012.

Gregoire, Carolyn. "The Surprising Link Between Gut Bacteria And Anxiety." Huffington Post. Science. 4 Jan. 2015. Web. 9 Jan. 2015.

Gross, Terry. "Habits: How They Form And How To Break Them." *NPR Fresh Air from WHYY*. 5 Mar. 2012. Web. 24 Jun. 2013.

Harrison, Lewis. *Healing Depression Naturally*. U.S.A.: Kensington, 2004. P. 63. Print.

Holick, Michael F. "Sunlight and vitamin D for bone health and prevention of autoimmune diseases, cancers, and cardiovascular disease." *The American Journal of Clinical Nutrition* 80.6 (Dec. 2004): 1678S-1688S. Web. 7 Sep. 2013.

"How Much Sleep Do We Really Need?" *National Sleep Foundation*. No Date. Web. 26 Mar 2012.

Hughes, Edward. "Art Therapy As A Healing Tool For Sub-Fertile Women." *Journal Of Medical Humanities* 31.1 (2010): 27-36. *Academic Search Premier*. Web. 2 Mar. 2012.

Jackson, Justine. "Animal-Assisted Therapy: The Human-Animal Bond In Relation To Human Health and Wellness." *Winona State University*. P. 7-8. Spring 2012. Web. 6 Dec 2014.

"Jessica Green: Are we filtering the wrong microbes?" Jessica Green. *Ted Talks*. Aug. 2011. Web. 17 Apr. 2012.

Johnson JM, Nachtigall Lb, and Stern TA. "The effect of testosterone levels on mood in men: a review." *Psychosomatics* 54.6 (2013 Nov-Dec): 509-14. *US National Library of Medicine. PubMed*. Web. 9 Jan. 2015. doi: 10.1016/j.psym.2013.06.018.

Jordan, Rob. "Stanford researchers find mental health prescription: Nature." Stanford Woods Institute for the Environment (30 Jun. 2015). Web. 26 Apr. 2018.

Judith Paice, et al. "Art Therapy For Relief Of Symptoms Associated With HIV/AIDS." *AIDS Care* 21.1 (2009): 64-69. *MEDLINE*. Web. 2 Mar. 2012.

Kemper, Kathi, and Suzanne Danhauer. "Music as Therapy." *Southern Medical Journal* 98.3 (2005): 282-288. *US National Library of Medicine. PubMed*. Web. 8 Dec. 2014.

Kim, Pilyoung, et al. "Effects of childhood poverty and chronic stress on emotion regulatory brain function in adulthood." Proceedings of the National Academy of Sciences of the United States of America (21 Oct. 2013). Web. 25 Oct. 2013. doi: 10.1073/pnas.1308240110

Klein, Sarah. "Inflammatory Foods: 9 Of The Worst Picks For Inflammation." *The Huffington Post*. 21 Mar. 2013. Web. 10 Jan. 2015.

Kresser, Chris. "Is Depression a Disease-or a Symptom of Inflammation?" *Chris Kresser*. Nov. 2014. Web. 11 Jan. 2015.

Law, Bridget M. "Probing the depression-rumination cycle." American Psychological Association. 36.10 (Nov. 2005): 38. Web. 15 Sep. 2013.

Layton, Julia. "Is it true that if you do anything for three weeks it will become a habit?" *howstuffworks*. No date. Web. 20 Jun. 2013.

Lienhard H, John. "No. 883: Smiles That Make You Happy." *Engines of Our Ingenuity. University of Houston*. No Date. Web. Apr 14, 2012.

Lokuge S, Frey BN, Foster JA, Soares CN, Steiner M. "Depression in women: windows of vulnerability and new insights into the link between estrogen and serotonin." *Journal of Clinical Psychiatry* 72.11 (Nov. 2011): e1563-9. Web. 10 Jan. 2015.

M Brown, et al. "Dampness And Mold In The Home And Depression: An Examination Of Mold-Related Illness And Perceived Control Of One's Home As Possible Depression Pathways." *American Journal Of Public Health* 97.10 (2007): 1893-1899. *CINAHL with Full Text*. Web. 22 Feb. 2012.

McGregor, Ian and Brian R. Little. "Personal Projects, Happiness, and Meaning: On Doing Well and Being Yourself." *Journal of Personality and Social Psychology* 74.2 (1998): 494-512. *US National Library of Medicine. National Center for Biotechnology Information*. Web. 14 Oct. 2013.

McLeod, S. A. "Short Term Memory." *Simply Psychology*. Web. 14 Dec. 2009. <https://www.simplypsychology.org/short-term-memory.html>.

"Meditation In Psychotherapy. An Ancient Spiritual Practice Is Finding New Uses In The Treatment Of Mental Illness." *The Harvard Mental Health Letter / From Harvard Medical School* 21.10 (2005): 1-4. *MEDLINE*. Web. 21 Feb. 2012.

Newitz, Annalee. "Eat a Lunch That Keeps You Productive All Afternoon." *Life Hacker*. 24 Aug. 2007. Web. 24 Feb. 2012.

Paula Goolkasian, et al. "Effects Of Brief And Sham Mindfulness Meditation On Mood And Cardiovascular Variables." *Journal Of Alternative & Complementary Medicine* 16.8 (2010): 867-873. *CINAHL with Full Text*. Web. 22 Feb. 2012.

procon.org. "Is medical marijuana an effective treatment for depression, bipolar disorders, anxiety, and similar mood disorders?" May 2005. Web. 8 Feb. 2012.

Rosenberg, Marshall. *Nonviolent Communication: A Language of Compassion*. Encinitas: Puddle Dancer Press, 2002. Print.

Ross J. Baldessarini, et al. "Coffee And Cigarette Use: Association With Suicidal Acts In 352 Sardinian Bipolar Disorder Patients." *Bipolar Disorders* 11.5 (2009): 494-503. *Academic Search Premier*. Web. 20 Feb. 2012.

Ruiz-Belda, María-Angeles, José-Miguel Fernández-Dols, and Kim Barchard. "Spontaneous Facial Expressions Of Happy Bowlers And Soccer Fans." *Cognition & Emotion* 17.2 (2003): 315. *Academic Search Premier*. Web. 15 Apr. 2012.

Russell Geen et al. "The Facilitation of Aggression by Aggression: Evidence against the Catharsis Hypothesis." *Journal of Personality and Social Psychology* 31.4 (Apr. 1975): 721-26. *US National Library of Medicine. National Institutes of Health*. Web. 13 Oct. 2013.

Scheel, KR, and JS Westefeld. "Heavy Metal Music and Adolescent Suicidality: An Empirical Investigation." *Adolescence* 34.134 (1999): 253-273.

Seligman ME, et al. "Positive psychology progress: empirical validation of interventions." *American Psychological Association* 60.5 (Jul.-Aug. 2005): 410-21. *US National Library of Medicine*. Web. 29 Oct. 2013.

Sinha R, Jastreboff AM. "Stress as a common risk factor for obesity and addiction." Biol Psychiatry. 2013;73(9):827–835.

Siple, Molly. "Anti-Inflammatory Diet." Natural Health Mag. The American Media. No Date. Web. 10 Jan. 2015.

Smith, Andrew P. and Amanda Wilds. "Effects of cereal bars for breakfast and mid-morning snacks on mood and memory." *International Journal of Food Sciences and Nutrition* 60.s4 (2009): 63-69. Web. 29 Dec. 2013. doi:10.1080/09637480802438305)

Smith, Melinda, et al. "How to Sleep Better." *HelpGuide.Org*. Dec. 2011. Web. 25 Feb. 2012.

Todd, Nivin. "Estrogen and Women's Emotions." *WebMD*. 31 May 2012. Web. 9 Jan. 2015.

Trapani, Gina. "Top 10 Ways to Sleep Smarter and Better." *Life Hacker*. 10 Oct. 2007. Web. 24 Feb. 2012.

Wright, Dr. Stephen. "Psychological Sense of Community: Theory of McMillan & Chavis (1986)." wright-house.com. Wright House, 2004. Web. 29 Jan. 2010.

ABOUT THE AUTHOR

Sage Liskey is an Oregon-born writer, artist, designer, and activist. He is the founder of the Rad Cat Press and author of zines and books covering mental health, activism, community, sustainability, and poetry. Follow his transformative work online at www.sageliskey.com

ABOUT THE ILLUSTRATOR

Barbara Counsil grew up among deciduous forests and drastically changing seasons of Northern Michigan. Now, she is constantly inspired by the juxtaposition of beauty and grit of the natural world. Barbara has been making art for ten years, with a BFA from Kendall College of Art and Design and a summer job as a park ranger assistant. Her combined passions in community art education and environmental stewardship have lead her to Sage Liskey, another wizarding warrior of health and peace. www.marbart.net

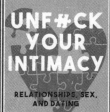
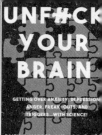